ZERO OIL SOUTH INDIAN COOK BOOK

OTHER BOOKS BY THE AUTHOR

ZERO OIL SOUTH INDIAN COOK BOOK

Dr. Bimal Chhajer M.D.

FUSION BOOKS

© Author

ISBN : 81-288-0512-6

Published by	: Fusion Books
	X-30, Okhla Industrial Area, Phase-II
	New Delhi-110020
Phone	: 011-41611861
Fax	: 011-41611866
E-mail	: sales@dpb.in
Website	: www.dpb.in
Edition	: 2008
Printed by	: Star Print-O-Bind, Okhla, New Delhi-20

ZERO OIL South Indian Cook Book
by *Dr. BIMAL CHHAJER M.D.*

Introduction to the Book

About twenty five percent of population of India are South Indians - supposed to be the descendants of the native Indians called Dravidians. Since the whole south India was surrounded by the sea – not much of influence was there from outside world on their language, cultures, customs and food. Then, depending on the local differences on the languages, the south Indians were divided into four states – Kerala, Tamil Nadu, Karnataka and Andhra Pradesh. Over the years - these south Indian foods were liked by other people of the country staying in east, north, west and central India and became popular. Today south Indians, wherever they have gone, have taken their recipes with them. In all, the south eastern countries, middle east and even in western countries, south Indian restaurants are popular.

As a part of the drive against consumption of oil and fatty items by the heart patients and health conscious persons- SAAOL – Science and art of living- program started preparing all the possible food items without any oil since 1995. We have so far successfully developed about 700 recipes – without any addition of oil but making each of them very tasty. Our recipe books called "Food for reversing heart Disease", "Zero oil cook book", "Zero oil sweets" and "Zero oil snacks" have already caused a revolution amongst health loving people. This particular book will add a new variety for those who are south Indians or those who love south Indian food.

Almost, majority of south Indian recipes are prepared with coconut oil – which is locally grown and popular. This is also probably one of the reasons that south Indians are getting more heart diseases. Addition of coconut – which is very high in oil content was also a problem in developing these recipes.

In the last so many years, when we started holding our heart reversal camps in Chennai, Bangalore and Hyderabad – the demand was to develop locally popular food. The hotel chefs were very helpful during these days and prepared for us lots of south Indian recipes. One of our south Indian dieticians , Subha Krishnan was specially helpful and she prepared about 20 recipes which I have used in this book. I must thank her for her help. Our other dietician Priyanka Rastogi was the one who made this possible to collect all the other recipes from different sources and from our patients. Many of my patients send me some of the recipes, specially Mrs Vasudeva of Mumbai. The photography was done by our colleague Nand Kishore, who also helped in the DTP and designing this book with Rajeev. Last but not the least, Aparna Kuna – one of our dieticians from Hyderabad- who is now doing her Ph.D from NIN, Hyderabad, also helped me to complete this book .I am very much indebted to all these people.

The recipes that are there in this book can be cooked even for a snack or for the meals. They can be modified – by adding some more spices or withdrawing some of the spices to suit your tongue. I am sure that this book will tremendously help many of the readers to follow SAAOL food, to prevent or reverse their heart disease.

About the Author

Dr. Bimal Chhajer, MD is the pioneering cardiologist who has developed "SAAOL Heart Program" – one of the most popular non-invasive heart care and treatment programs in India. Dr. Chhajer, 41, hails from Rajasthan but has grown up in Kolkata. He conceptualized the concept of bringing all the possible, useful items together – be it from Science or Art – to treat heart patients. His insight has helped thousands of patients to cure themselves without going for Bypass Surgery or Angioplasty, without any risk.

He has worked as an Assistant Professor at the All India Institute of Medical Sciences (AIIMS) and carried out his research work at AIIMS for six years when he developed the program. He also represented AIIMS at the eleventh Antartica Expedition from India.

He has not only lectured all over India and the world, but has been in the field of cardiology for more than 15 years. He has also authored eight books :

1. Reversal of Heart Disease in Five easy steps
2. Food for Reversing Heart Disease
3. Hriday Rog se Mukti
4. Understanding Heart Disease
5. Hriday Rog Samanya Jankari
6. Zero Oil Sweet Book (English & Hindi)
7. Zero Oil Cook Book (English & Hindi)
8. Zero Oil Namkeen Book (English & Hindi)

A Book on "201 Diet Tips" is in the pipeline. He also brings out a monthly journal "Heart Talk" covering a wide range of heart related topics. His writing is very easy to read and understand. More than 600 articles have been written in magazines and newspapers about him and SAAOL Heart Program. He has regularly appeared in TV programs, news and talks. He is considered a Pioneer in Preventive and Non-Invasive Cardiology in India.

SAAOL Heart Program training is now held regularly in all the major cities of India, including Delhi, Kolkata, Mumbai, Chennai, Bangalore and Hyderabad. Dr. Chhajer organized the first international conference, in conjunction with AIIMS on **"Life Style and Heart"** in 1995 and 2nd International Conference on **"Life Style and Health"** in November 1999, at India Habitat Center, New Delhi .

Dr. Chhajer has been awarded with "Rajeev Gandhi Akta Puraskar, 2002" and "Bhasker Award, 2002". He was also chosen for "Rotary International Vocational Award in 2002". His "Zero Oil" cooking method has created a revolution in cooking method all over the country.

Why Zero Oil?

The commonest form of lifestyle, which people have in this modern era, is sedentary lifestyle. Very few are involved in regular physical activity. Most of us have a lifestyle which has minimal of physical work, no exercise and bad dietary habits i.e. sedentary lifestyle.

Now, it is known to all, that fat forms blockages in the arteries (tubes which carry blood) like coronary arteries. These fats are called cholesterol and triglycerides. They get deposited in layers over a period of years. When these blockages become significant, the tubes (arteries) get choked leading to a disease called coronary artery disease (angina, heart attack).

In the past 50 years cholesterol (an animal fat) was considered as the only constituent of the blockages. It was only in the last one decade or so, that triglyceride (a plant fat) has been found to be equally responsible for creating blockages. Triglyceride is the chemical name, known to the common man as "Cooking Oil". The oil manufacturing companies exploited the innocence of the people, misled them to believe that oils are harmless by promoting their sales with captions like "Cholesterol Free" or "Zero cholesterol Oil". Well, it is true that oil does not have cholesterol because it is made from plant seeds, whereas cholesterol comes from animal products (meat, milk & their products). The lay men started buying these oils. What they failed to realize was that these oils are also hundred percent fats because they are triglycerides and triglycerides are equally harmful. Oils also have high calories content (each gram gives nine calories) that can lead to obesity, diabetes and high blood pressure. It is best to minimize the fat content in our food (optimum requirement of fat by the body is 10% of the total calories).

This can be easily obtained from all the food items, as every food contains oil known as invisible fat or hidden fat. This means that all the visible sources of fat (i.e. cooking oil) should be completely cut down. Now, this would raise a query: How to prepare delicious food without oil?

What if the food is prepared without oil? Will the taste be there? If you think rationally, the answer would be yes. The taste comes from the spices (Masalas). Oil itself does not add taste. It is our mindset, which was trained to believe all these years, which says that taste comes from oil. But when we ask to remove the oil, the masalas get removed automatically. This happens because the housewife does not know how to put the spices, when no oil appears in the frying pan. This prompted SAAOL to develop the concept of "Zero Oil". By "Zero Oil", we mean cooking without using a single drop of oil. SAAOL cooks the spices and food in water and since the spices are there, the colour, taste and flavour remains intact.

SAAOL also realizes that the mindset of people finds it difficult to accept water as the cooking media. So we have named water, when used as cooking media – "SAAOL Oil". By introducing the zero oil concept in your cooking, there will be no risk of taking in cholesterol & triglycerides. This can also be helpful in reducing weight, since the high calorie gain from fat is removed.

We can now aptly say that SAAOL Oil contains no fat, no cholesterol, is 100% mineral and good for health.

The Concept of SAAOL

SAAOL is a Rajasthani (Marwardi) word which means "**to do things in the best possible way**". SAAOL is an acronym for "Science and Art of Living".

SAAOL Heart Program

SAAOL Heart Program is a three day training program for heart patients and their families, conducted by Dr. Bimal Chhajer all over India. The entire theoretical concept of SAAOL is delivered practically one to one during the training program by a team of Doctors, Diet specialists, Yoga instructors and Heart specialists. Food is one of the most important components of SAAOL and none of them contains any oil. The training consists of medical drug treatment combined with dietary modification, yoga, meditation and management of stress. This scientific process leading to reversal of blockages, has been tried by more than 6000 patients successfully all over India. These training programs are regularly conducted in all the metro cities of India (Delhi, Kolkata, Hyderabad, Mumbai, Chennai). In Delhi this program is conducted every month and in Kolkata, Hyderabad, Mumbai, Chennai after every third month. This program helps people to avoid Bypass Surgery and Angioplasty. Those who have undertaken surgeries can also avoid reblockages by the same process. Heart Attacks can also be avoided.

For further enquires and information booklet please contact :

Head Office :
SAAOL Heart Centre
14/84-85, Vikram Vihar, Lajpat Nagar - IV, New Delhi - 110024
Tel.: 26235168, 26283098, 26211908   Fax: 26212016   Email:
info@saaol.com, bimalkc@nde.vsnl.net.in   Website: www.saaol.com

KOLKATA
Co-ordinator - Mr. Rajesh Jain
210/A, Rash Bihari Avenue,
Gariahat Crossing, Kolkata - 700029
Tel.: 24641140, 27021244 Mob. No. : 9831153008

CHENNAI
Co-ordinator - Mr. K. Chhajer
C/o Jeans Park India Pvt. Ltd,
566, Anna Salai, Chennai - 600018
Tel.: 22260209, 22260935

MUMBAI
Co-ordinator - Mr. Deepak Dalal
B-301, Gold Mist, Thakur Complex,
Kandivli (E), Mumbai - 400101
Tel.: 56995378, 28543088 Fax: 28544217

BANGALORE
Co-ordinator-Mr. S.S. Prasad
25, S.P. Road, Off. 4th Temple Street,
Malleswaram, Bangalore - 560003
Tel.: 56993797, 3462869, 3310856, 36736554 (Reliance)

HYDERABAD
Co-ordinator - Mr. S.L.Chhajer
Sarda Adeifice, Flat No. 203, H.No. - 3-5-590, Vittalwadi,
Himayat Nagar, Hyderabad - 500029
Tel.: 23224084

Oils & Its Composition

Fat is present naturally in many foods as invisible fat. Visible fats are made from products like Ghee, Butter, Cooking Oil, Salad Oil, and Margarine. Oils that have a relatively high melting point and are solid at room temperature are called Fats. Whereas those that have lower melting points and are liquid at room temperature are called oils.

Fats (Triglycerides) are concentrated sources of energy. They reduce bulk in the diet. Fats are slow in leaving the stomach and hence retard digestion. (1gm of fat gives 9 calories).

All fat is comprised of three components in varying proportions. Saturated fat, Mono-unsaturated & Poly-unsaturated.

Although many people believe that adding olive oil or safflower oil to their food will lower their cholesterol levels, this is unfortunately not true. Adding any oil to your food will raise your cholesterol level.

The reason being while some oils are higher in Saturated fat than others, all oils contain some S.F., so the more oil you eat, the more S.F. you consume. Diet high in saturated fats will cause obesity, slows digestion and absorption of essential nutrients and can ultimately cause cardiovascular disease. Saturated fats have an ability to thicken the blood and thus increase its tendency to clot.

Some foods have high quantities of invisible saturated fats and so should be avoided in diet, such as whole milk, eggs, meat, fish, cheese.

The dietary habits we people grow up with, are responsible in part for the development of cardiovascular diseases.

Although some amount of cholesterol is essential for a healthy body as it circulates in the blood and is found in nerve tissues, liver, kidneys, brain, adrenal gland and also in mother's milk. However, in excess it becomes harmful. A surplus of cholesterol in diet causes fatty streaks to appear in the blood, even among people who appear healthy or slim. These fatty streaks narrow the arteries by sticking to its lining and this may further cause hypertension, angina, heart attack and stroke. So to prevent this, one must reduce the intake of all fats and avoid all animal products.

Composition of Oils: % age fatty acid composition
(Approximate value)

Oil	Saturated	Mono Unsaturated	Poly Unsaturated
Cotton oil	91	8	1
Cotton Seed Oil	34	26	40
Ground Nut Oil	20	54	26
Mustard Oil	6	73	21
Palm Oil	80	13	7
Safflower Oil	11	13	76
Sesame	14	46	40
Soyabean	15	25	60
Sunflower	8	34	58
Corn Oil	17	3.4	7.9
Olive Oil	1.9	98	1.2
Coconut Oil	11.7	0.8	0.2
Peanut Oil	2.6	6.2	4.1
Canola Oil (Puritan)	0.8	8.4	4.4

Preferred Methods of Cooking

India has a tradition of cooking food with lots of oil, which is to be avoided by heart patients. So, our methods of cooking are :

ROASTING: Roasting and baking are essentially the same. They are carried out in an oven between temperatures of 120^0 C and 260^0 C. Generally, the term roasting is applied to papad, while baking is used for breads, cakes and biscuits. The food is cooked partially by dry heat and partially by moist heat, if the food is high in moisture content. In baking, the oven atmosphere should be moist initially, so that the moisture condenses on the cold dough. This helps in heat transfer and plays a part in the formation of crust. Roasting and Baking involve heat transfer from the heat source in the oven by radiation, conduction and convection. Heat is transferred directly onto the container of the food through which it is conducted to the food. Convection currents of air help keep the temperature of the oven fairly uniform. This process has an advantage that it does not involve oil and the most important thing is that the food is cooked properly with plenty of taste.

BOILING: Boiling involves cooking in water. In this, the medium transferring heat is water. Water receives heat by conduction through the sides of the utensils in which the food is cooked and passes on the heat by convection currents, which equalize the temperature and become very vigorous when boiling commences. Water is a poor conductor of heat and its heat capacity is high, i.e. it requires more heat than any other liquid of the same weight to raise the temperature. The boiling point of water is 100^0 C and it is altered at high altitudes and in presence of electrolytes.

STEAMING: Steam is the medium of cooking in steam, "waterless" cooking and pressure-cooking. Cooking by these methods involves moist heat. In steaming, food is cooked by steam from added water, whilst in waterless cooking, the steam originates from the food itself. Pressure-cooking is a device to reduce the cooking time by increasing the pressure so that the boiling point of water is automatically raised. While water boils at 100^0 C at normal atmospheric pressure, it boils at 121^0 C at a pressure of 1.07 kg/cm^2, which is the pressure at which food is cooked in a kitchen pressure cooker. In cooking by steam, the food is heated as a result of steam condensing on the food, and the release of the large quantity of heat contained in the steam. This continues until the heated food reaches the same temperature as steam.

Zero Oil Way of Frying

1. Heat a kadhai (preferably non-stick pan).
2. Dry roast the jeera (cumin seeds) until it crackles and turns brown.
3. Add ground onion in the kadhai (non-stick pan) and keep roasting it. When it starts sticking upon the hot surface, add small amount of water and keep stiring.
4. Add ginger and garlic paste (according to your taste/wish).
5. Roast the onion, ginger, garlic till it turns to brown. (Note : Do not add more water at a time as it gives the food – a boiled taste.
6. Then add tomato paste in the kadhai and roast it with little amount of water.
7. Roast till the water bubbles start forming.
8. Add the turmeric powder and cook for sometime (as turmeric takes time in cooking).
9. Finally add all the masalas/spices like salt, red chilli powder and coriander powder according to the taste.
10. Now, the zero oil masala is ready.
11. If you want to make vegetables – add vegetables, if you wish to cook dal – add boiled dal or soaked dal. Cook as required.
12. Add garam masala (A combination of cloves, mace, nutmeg, black cardamom, red chillies).
13. Garnish it with finely chopped coriander leaves.

Introduction To
South Indian Culinary

Indian food is as diverse as its culture, its religions, geography, climatic conditions and traditions. All of these combine to influence the preparation of Indian food. Essentially spicy, the cuisine is, however, not always hot. It is the different combination of a handful of spices that produce the most delectable dishes. In India, preparation of food is an art, perfected over time and passed through generations by just word of mouth. Food is also an important part of Indian festivals and traditions; no celebration is complete without a feast. Special preparations are a must during festivals.

Speaking of the variety of Indian dishes, south Indian and north Indian dishes vary in style. South Indian cusine is rice based. South Indian dishes are inclined to be more hot and spicy. The south Indian specialties include Idli, Dosa, Sambar and rice accompanied with a variety of dishes. These items are glorious and delicious, besides being nourishing and digestible (due to the fermenting process). Coconut is a major ingredient of the south Indian dishes. The 'Roti' or 'Chappatis' or 'Parathas' accompanied with a wide assortment of "curries", which include spicy vegetables and lentils is the typical north Indian food.

A typical traditional meal in South India is served on a freshly cut plantain leaf. The food that is served on a banana leaf is displayed like an identity card.

CUISINE OF ANDHRA PRADESH

Andhra Pradesh has often been called the "food bowl of South India". The cuisine of Andhra Pradesh is reputedly the spiciest and hottest of all Indian cuisine. Rice, the staple Andhra food, is served with sambar and other lentil preparations along with vegetables.

This includes both, the original Andhra cooking and the Hyderabadi cuisine with its Mughlai influence. The food is very delicious and spices are used liberally in their food.

CUISINE OF KARNATAKA

Karnataka's culinary culture revolves round three staple items- rice, 'ragi' and 'jowar'. The popular 'BisiBela Bath', 'Uppittu' and 'Holighe' are the delicious and popular food items from this region. Many factors and influences have contributed to enrich this culinary heritage. Though there are many similarities between the food of Karnataka and its southern neighbours, the typical Mysore cuisine is well known for its own distinctive textural forms and flavour, with the dishes complementing and balancing each other.

The cuisine of Karnataka as any other Indian cuisine, is influenced by both Hindu and Muslim traditions brought by the different rulers of this region. The culinary fare offered by Karnataka is quite varied with each region of the state, having its own unique flavours.

CUISINE OF TAMILNADU

Tamilnadu is the land of the delicious Pongal, hot Idli and Sambar, spicy Puliogare, and the popular dosa. Tamilians are essentially rice-eating people and they have preparations made of rice for all the meals of the day. Lentils too are consumed extensively, as accompaniment to the rice preparations. While tamarind is used for adding that distinctive tang, peppercorns and chillies, both green and red, are used to make the food hot. To neutralize the effect of the chillies, and soothe the stomach curd is used in a variety of dishes. Other spices like mustard, cumin garlic etc. are used for tempering and seasoning.

CUISINE OF KERALA

The unusual cuisine of Kerala brings to the fore, the culinary expertise of the people of Kerala. Producing some of the tastiest foods on earth the people of Kerala are gourmets with a difference. The cuisine is very hot and spicy and offers several gastronomic opportunities Keralites are mostly rice eating people. The foods in this land are rich with coconut, though one can't imagine Kerala food without chillies curry leaf, mustard seed, tamarind and asafoetida. Keralites put to good use, whatever the land offers and the result is a marvellous cuisine that is simple yet palate tickling.

In this book, we have tried to use less and less of coconut because they are full of fat which is not good for heart diseases. Whereve coconut chutney is used, we have used dhal chutney. Usage of mustar in the recipes has been cut down to the minimal quantities, to reduc the fat content of the recipes. The book offers innumerable dishe varying in taste, style and method. So try out these zero oil south India foods which are a brilliant blend of flavours, colours, seasoning, nutrition balance, fragrance, taste and visual appeal.

Contents

SNACKS

SWEET DISHES

CHUTNEYS AND PICKLES

BASIC RECEIPES

Ingredients

- 1 cup mixed vegetables (radish, potato, onion, ladies fingers, brinjal, capsicum), cut into ½ inch piece
- 2 green chillies slit sideways
- ½ cup red gram dhal
- 3 teaspoon sambhar powder
- ½ teaspoon turmeric powder
- 2 cups water
- 1 tablespoon rice flour
- lemon sized tamarind
- salt to taste
- 1 small bunch coriander leaves, for garnishing

For Tempering

- 1 teaspoon mustard seeds
- ½ teaspoon asafoetida powder
- ½ teaspoon fenugreek seeds
- ½ teaspoon cumin seeds
- 1 red chilli halved
- a few curry leaves

METHOD

1. Cook the red gram dhal in a pressure cooker and set aside

2. Soak the tamarind in 1 cup of water and extract the juice

3. Heat Karahi and add all the ingredients for tempering. When the mustard seeds splutter, add the slit green chillies and the chopped vegetables.

4. Add the tamarind juice, the remaining one cup of water, salt, turmeric and sambar powder. Close with a lid and cook till the vegetables are cooked

5. Add the cooked red gram dhal and simmer for five more minutes, till every thing blends well.

6. If the sambar needs to be thickened, make a smooth paste of the rice flour in 2 tablespoons of water and add to the sambar and cook for another two to three minutes, till the raw smell disappears.

7. Garnish with chopped coriander leaves. Serve hot with rice.

Small Onion Sambar
(Vengaya Sambar)

Ingredients
- 1 kg small sambar onions
- ½ cup red gram dhal
- 3 teaspoons sambhar powder
- ½ teaspoon turmeric powder
- lemon sized tamarind
- salt to taste
- 1 small bunch coriander leaves, for garnishing

For Paste
- ½ teaspoon fenugreek seeds
- 6 red chillies
- ½ teaspoon asafoetida powder
- 1 teaspoon cumin seeds
- 3 tablespoon coriander seeds
- 1½ tablespoon bengal gram dal
- 2 teaspoon poppy seeds

For Tempering
- 1 teaspoon mustard seeds
- ½ teaspoon fenugreek seeds
- ½ teaspoon cumin seeds
- 1 red chilli halved
- a few curry leaves

METHOD

1. Skin onions and set aside

2. Soak tamarind in 1 ½ cups of water and extract the juice and set aside

3. Pressure cook the dhal and set aside

4. **To Make The Paste:** Roast the 2 teaspoon of fenugreek seeds, red chillies, asafoetida, cumin seeds, coriander seeds, bengal gram dhal and poppy seeds. Grind to a fine paste and add the 4 –6 small sambar onions. Use very little water. Set aside

5. Heat karahi and add all the ingredients of tempering. When the mustard seeds splutter, add the sambar onions and roast on a low heat for about five minutes.

6. Add the tamarind juice, turmeric powder and salt. Cover and simmer for five to seven minutes till the raw smell disappears.

7. Add the cooked dhal and ground masala paste and cook for another five minutes till every thing blends well.If the sambar is too thick,add ¼ cup water and bring to the boil.

8. Garnish with the chopped coriander leaves

9. Serve hot with rice

3 | Butter Milk Kuzhambu
(Moru Khuzhambu)

Ingredients

- 1 cup ashgourd, chopped to ½ inch size
- 1 teaspoon red gram dhal
- 1 teaspoon Bengal gram dhal
- ½ inch piece ginger shredded fine
- 2 teaspoon cumin seeds
- 1 tablespoon coriander seeds
- 6 green chillies
- ½ teaspoon turmeric powder
- 2 cups well mixed curd
- salt to taste

For Tempering

- 1 teaspoon mustard seeds
- 1 teaspoon fenugreek seeds
- 1 red chilli halved
- ½ teaspoon asafoetida powder
- a few curry leaves

METHOD

1. Soak in ½ cup water, the red gram dhal and Bengal gram dhal for an hour.
2. Grind to a fine paste all the soaked dhals, ginger, cumin seeds, coriander seeds, green chillies, using very little water.
3. Add the ground paste to the curd. Add the salt and turmeric powder. Mix well and set aside
4. Heat karahi and add all the ingredients for tempering. When the mustard seeds splutter, add the chopped ash gourd. Pour enough water to cover the vegetables. Cover with a lid and simmer on a low heat till done
5. Add the curd mixture to the vegetable and heat thorough. Take care to prevent curdling
6. Serve hot with rice.

4

Pepper Kuzhambu
(Milagu Kuzhambu)

Ingredients
- 1 big lemon size tamarind
- a few curry leaves
- salt to taste

Masala
- 1 ¼ tablespoon peppercorns
- 1¼ tablespoons Bengal gram dhal
- 1 teaspoon coriander seeds
- 2 red chillies
- ½ teaspoon asafoetida powder

For Tempering
- 1 teaspoon mustard seeds

METHOD

1. Soak the tamarind in 2 cups of water and extract the juice and set aside.

2. Dry roast the ingredients for the masala and powder fine. Add the little water and make a paste. Set aside.

3. Heat karahi and add the mustard seeds. When they splutter, add the tamarind juice and salt

4. Close the lid and simmer on a low heat till the raw smell disappears

5. Add the masala paste and bring to a boil.

6. Just before turning of the heat add the curry leaves.

7. Serve hot with rice.

5

Spicy Tamarind Kuzhambu
(Vatral Kuzhambu)

Ingredients

- Lemon sized tamarind
- 150 gms small sambar onions, skinned
- 3 teaspoons sambar powder
- 2 tablespoons jaggry, powdered
- 2 tablespoons bengal gram flour
- Salt to taste

For Tempering

- 3 tablespoons gingelly oil
- 2 red chillies, halved
- 1 teaspoon mustard seeds
- 1 teaspoon red gram dhal
- 1 teaspoon bengal gram dhal
- 1 teaspoon black gram dhal
- ½ teaspoon fenugreek seeds
- ½ teaspoon asafoetida powder
- A few curry leaves

METHOD

1. Soak the tamarind in 2 cups water and extract the juice. Set aside.

2. Heat karahi and add the mustard seeds red chillies, asafoetida powder and fenugreek seeds. When the mustard seeds splutter, add the red gram dhal, bengal gram dhal, black gram dhal and the curry leaves. Roast till the dhal turns golden.

3. Add the onions and roast for a couple of minutes.

4. Add the sambar powder. Roast for a minute.

5. Add the tamarind juice, salt and jaggery. Close with a lid and simmer on a low heat for about ten minutes till the raw smell of the tamarind disappears.

6. Meanwhile make a batter of medium consistency with the bengal gram flour in half a cup of water. Add to the kuzhambu. Boil for a couple of minutes.

7. Serve hot with rice.

Dumpling Kuzhambu
(Parupu Urundai Kuzhambu)

6

Ingredients
Lemon sized tamarind

3 teaspoons sambar powder,

2 tablespoons jaggery, powdered

Salt to taste

For the Dumplings
1 cup red gram dhal, 4-6 red chillies

½ teaspoon asafoetida powder, salt to taste

For Tempering
1 teaspoon mustard seeds

½ teaspoon fenugreek seeds

2 red chillies, halved

½ teaspoon asafoetida powder

1 teaspoon black gram dhal

1 teaspoon bengal gram dhal

1 teaspoon red gram dhal

A few curry leaves

METHOD

1. Soak the tamarind in 2 cups water and extract the juice. Set aside.

2. To make the dumplings : Soak the red gram dhal and red chillies in water for a couple of hours and grind to a thick paste, adding the asafoetida powder and salt.

3. Heat a karahi, add a few curry leaves and the ground paste. Fry

for a couple of minutes. Turn off the heat and shape into small balls.

4. Place the balls on an idli stand and steam in a pressure cooker (without the weight) for about ten minutes. Set aside and cool.

5. In the meantime, heat a karahi and add the mustard seeds, red chillies, fenugreek seeds, curry leaves and asafoetida powder. When the mustard seeds splutter, add the black gram dhal, Bengal gram dhal, red gram dhal and roast till golden.

6. Add the sambar powder and roast for a minute.

7. Add the tamarind juice, salt and jaggery, close with a lid and simmer for ten minutes till the raw smell of the tamarind disappears.

8. Add the steamed dhal dumplings and simmer for another ten minutes.

9. Serve hot with rice.

(Famous in Tamil Nadu)

7 | Mysore Kuzhambu

Ingredients
- ¼ kg beans, chopped to ½ inch pieces
- 2 tablespoons shelled peas
- 1 potato, chopped to ½ inch pieces
- ¼ cup red gram dhal
- ½ teaspoon turmeric powder
- Salt to taste

Paste
- 1 tablespoon coriander seeds
- 1 teaspoon mustard seeds
- 1 tablespoon raw rice
- 6 red chillies
- ½ teaspoon asafoetida powder

For Tempering
- 1 teaspoon mustard seeds
- 1 teaspoon cummin seeds
- 1 red chilli, halved
- A few curry leaves

METHOD
1. Pressure cook the red gram dhal and set aside.
2. Grind fine all the ingredients for the paste, using very little water. Set aside.
3. Add enough water to cover the vegetables and cook till done.
4. Add the dhal, salt, turmeric powder, and the paste. Simmer on a low heat till everything blends.
5. Heat a pan and add all the ingredients for tempering. When the mustard seeds splutter, add to the kuzhambu.
6. Serve hot with rice.

8 | Cauliflower Kuzhambu
(Cauliflower Poritha Kuzhambu)

Ingredients

- ½ cup red gram dhal
- 2 cups cauliflower (1 medium size)
- Chopped into flowerets
- 2 tomotoes, quartered
- ½ teaspoons sambar powder
- 2 teaspoons rice flour
- ½ teaspoon turmeric powder
- Salt to taste

Paste

- 1 teaspoon coriander seeds
- ½ teaspoon peppercorns
- 1 teaspoon black gram dhal
- ½ teaspoon asafoetida powder

For Tempering

- 1 teaspoon mustard seeds
- 1 teaspoon black gram dhal
- 1 red chilli, halved
- A few curry leaves

METHOD

1. Pressure cook the red gram dhal and set aside.
2. Roast all the ingredients for the paste. Adding very little water.

3. Dissolve the 2 teaspoons rice flour in ½ cup water. Set aside.

4. Cook the chopped cauliflower in sufficient water, adding the tomatoes, sambar powder, turmeric powder and salt. Simmer till the vegetables are tender.

5. Add the ground paste, the dissolved rice, flour and the cooked dhal. Simmer till everything blends well.

6. Heat a karahi and add all the ingredients for tempering. When the mustard seeds splutter, add to the kuzhambu.

7. Serve hot with rice.

9

Bitter Gourd Pitlay
(Paavakkai Pitlay)

Ingredients

- 2-3 medium sized bitter gourds (125 gm) chopped fine
- 1 tomato, chopped fine
- ½ cup red gram dhal
- 1 tablespoon powdered jaggery
- 2 teaspoons sambar powder
- ½ teaspoon turmeric powder
- Lemon sized tamarind
- 2 ½ cups water
- Salt to taste

Paste

- 6 red chillies
- 1 tablespoon coriander seeds
- ½ teaspoon peppercorns
- 1 teaspoon bengal gram dhal
- 1 teaspoon black gram dhal
- ½ teaspoon asafoetida powder

For Tempering

- 1 teaspoon mustard seeds
- A few curry leaves

METHOD

1. Pressure-cook the red gram dhal. Set aside.
2. Soak the tamarind in 1-cup water and extract the juice. Set aside.
3. Roast the ingredients for the paste. Grind to a fine paste.
4. Heat the tamarind juice and add the chopped bitter gourd, salt, sambar powder, turmeric powder, and jaggery. Simmer on a low heat till the vegetable is done.
5. Add the chopped tomato and the ground paste and simmer for a couple of minutes. Add the cooked dhal and simmer till well blended.   .
6. Heat the karahi and add the mustard seeds and curry leaves. When the mustard seeds splutter, add to the pitlay.
7. Serve hot with rice.

10 Curry Leaves Kuzhambu
(Karivepilai Kuzhambu)

Ingredients
For Paste
- 5-6 red chillies
- 1 teaspoon asafoetida powder
- 2 teaspoons black gram dhal
- 1 ½ teaspoons raw rice
- Lemon-sized tamarind
- About 30 curry leaves
- Salt to taste

For Tempering
- 1 teaspoon mustard seeds
- ¼ teaspoon fenugreek seeds
- 1 red chilli, halved

METHOD

1. Roast dry the red chillies, peppercorns, asafoetida powder, black gram dhal and rice. Add the curry leaves and tamarind, grind to a fine paste. Use very little water.

2. Dissolv the ground paste in 2 cups of water add salt and set aside.

3. Heat the karahi. Add the ingredients for tempering. When the mustard seeds splutter, add the dissolved paste and simmer till the kuzhambu thickens.

4. Serve hot with rice and roasted papads.

   This spicy, thick kuzhambu must be eaten with a greater quantity of rice than is usual with other kuzhambu.

Mashed Green Gram Dhal
(Payatham Paruppu Masial)

11

Ingredients
- 1 cup green gram dhal
- 6 green chillies, slit sideways
- ½ teaspoon turmeric powder
- Lemon-sized tamarind
- Small bunch coriander leaves, chopped fine
- Salt to taste

For Tempering
- 1 teaspoon mustard seeds
- 1 red chilli, halved
- ½ teaspoon asafoetida powder
- A few curry leaves

METHOD

1. Pressure cook the green gram dhal. Set aside.

2. Soak the tamarind in 1 cup of water and extract the juice. Set aside.

3. Heat the karahi, add all the ingredients for tempering. When the mustard seeds splutter, add the green chillies, tamarind juice, turmeric powder and salt. Simmer till the raw smell of the tamarind disappers.

4. Add the cooked dhal. Simmer till everything blends well.

5. Garnish with chopped coriander leaves.

6. Serve hot with rice or chapattis.

12 Tarmarind Kodayal
(Pulli Kodayal)

Ingredients
- 200 gms ash gourd, chopped to ½ inch piece
- 2 green chillies, slit sideways
- 1 tablespoon grated jaggery
- lemon sized tamarind
- a bunch of coriander leaves,
- Chopped fine for garnishing
- Salt to taste

Ground Paste
- 6-8 red chillies
- ¼ teaspoon fenugreek seeds
- 1 teaspoon white sesame seeds
- 1 tablespoon bengal gram dhal
- 1 tablespoon black gram dhal
- 1 tablespoon coriander seeds.
- ½ teaspoon asafoetida powder

For Tempering
- 1 teaspoon mustard seeds
- 1 teaspoon black gram dhal
- 1 red chilli, halved
- A few curry leaves.

METHOD

1. **To make the paste :** Roast the remaining ingredients till the dhals turn golden. Grind to a fine paste adding, tamarind and some water. Set aside.

2. Heat karahi and add all the ingredients for tempering. When the mustard seeds splutter, add the chopped ash gourd, salt and 2 cups of water. Cover and simmer till the vegetables are done.

3. Add the slit green chillies paste, powdered jaggery and simmer till everything blends well.

4. Garnish with chopped coriander leaves.

5. Serve hot with rice.

Tomato Rasam
(Thakkali Rasam)

13

Ingredients
- 4 large tomatoes, chopped fine
- 3 tablespoons red gram dhal
- 3 green chillies, slit sideways
- 1" piece ginger, chopped fine
- ½ teaspoon turmeric powder
- 2 ½ cups water, salt to taste
- Chopped coriander leaves for garnishing

For Tempering
- 2 teaspoon mustard seeds
- 1 teaspoon cumin seeds
- 1 red chilli, halved
- 1 teaspoon powdered pepper
- ½ teaspoon asafoetida powder
- A few curry leaves

METHOD

1. Pressure cook the red gram dhal and set aside.
2. Heat karahi and add all the ingredients for tempering. When the mustard seeds splutter, add the green chillies, ginger and tomatoes.
3. Add 1 up of water, salt and turmeric powder. Allow to simmer for five minutes.
4. Add the cooked dhal and the remaining 1½ cups water and bring to the boil.
5. Garnish with chopped coriander leaves. Serve hot.

14 Lemon Rasam
(Elumichampazha Rasam)

Ingredients

- Juice of 1 lemon
- ¼ cup red gram dhal
- 2 tomatoes, quartered
- 4 green chillies
- 1-inch piece ginger, scraped and shredded
- ¾ teaspoon peppercorns
- ½ teaspoon cumin seeds
- ½ teaspoon turmeric powder
- 1 ½ cups water
- 1 small bunch coriander leaves, chopped fine for garnishing
- Salt to taste

For Tempering

- 1 teaspoon mustard seeds
- ½ teaspoon asafoetida powder
- 1 red chilli, halved
- A few curry leaves

METHOD

1. Pressure cook the red gram dhal. Set aside.
2. Grind together the ginger and green chillies. Set aside.
3. Powder the cumin seeds and peppercorns. Set aside.
4. Add to the cooked dhal, 1 ½ cups water, salt, turmeric powder, ginger-chilli paste and bring to the boil on a low heat.

5. Heat karahi and add all the ingredients for tempering. Add also the pepper-cummin seed powder. When the mustard seeds splutter, add to the rasam. Turn off the heat.

6. Add the lemon juice. Garnish with chopped coriander leaves.

7. Serve hot with rice.

15 Ginger Rasam
(Inji Rasam)

Ingredients

- 3 tablespoons red gram dhal
- 3-4 teaspoons cumin seeds
- 1 teaspoon peppercorns
- 3 green chillies
- 2-3 pieces ginger (1-inch long)
- 1 tablespoon jaggery, powdered
- Chopped coriander leaves for garnishing
- Salt to taste

For Tempering

- 1 teaspoon mustard seeds
- 1 teaspoon cumin seeds
- ½ teaspoon asafoetida powder
- 1 red chilli halved
- A few curry leaves

METHOD

1. Soak the red gram dhal in 1 cup of water for ½ an hour.

2. Grind the cumin seeds, peppercorns, green chillies, ginger, and jaggery to a fine paste, adding the soaked dhal.

3. Add ½ cups of water and salt to the ground paste and bring to the boil.

4. Simmer on a low heat for a couple of minutes. Add some more water if the rasam is too thick.

5. Heat karahi and roast all the ingredients for tempering. When the mustard seeds splutter, add to the rasam.

6. Garnish with chopped coriander leaves. Serve hot.

16 Cumin Seed Pepper Rasam
(Jeera-Milagu Rasam)

Ingredients
- 3 tablespoons red gram dhal
- 3-4 teaspoons cumin seeds
- 1 teaspoon red gram dhal
- 1 red chilli
- ½ teaspoon asafoetida powder
- lemon-sized tamarind
- Salt to taste
- For tempering
- 1 teaspoon mustard seeds
- ½ teaspoon cumin seeds
- 1 red chilli, halved
- A few curry leaves

METHOD
1. Soak the tamarind in 1 cup of water and extract the juice.
2. Roast the peppercorns, cumin seeds, red gram dhal, red chilli and asafoetida powder and grind fine. Set aside.
3. Heat karahi and add all the ingredients for tempering. When the mustard seeds splutter, add the tamarind juice and salt. Simmer for a few minutes till the raw smell of the tamarind disappears.
4. Add the ground powder and simmer for a couple of minutes.
5. Serve hot with rice.

17 | Garlic Rasam
(Poondu Rasam)

Ingredients
- 20-25 garlic cloves
- Lemon-sized tamarind
- Salt to taste

Paste
- ¾ teaspoon peppercorns
- 4 red chillies
- 2 teaspoons coriander seeds
- 1 teaspoon Bengal gram dhal
- 1 teaspoon cumin seeds
- A few curry leaves

For Tempering
- 1 teaspoon mustard seeds
- 2 red chillies, halved

METHOD

1. **To make the paste** : Heat karahi and roast red chillies, peppercorns, coriander seeds and bengal gram dhal. Grind into a fine paste, adding the raw cumin seeds and curry leaves. Set aside.
2. Soak the tamarind in 2 cups of water and extract the juice. Add the salt and simmer on a low heat till the raw smell of the tamarind disappears.
3. In the meantime, roast garlic cloves and add to the boiling tamarind juice.
4. Add the ground paste. Simmer till everything blends well. Add more water if the rasam is too thick.
5. Heat karahi and add all the ingredients for tempering. When the mustard seeds splutter, add to the rasam.
6. Serve hot.

(Famous in Tamil Nadu)

18 | Buttermilk Rasam
(Moru Rasam)

Ingredients
- 1 cup sour buttermilk
- ¼ cup red gram dhal
- 1 tomato, quartered
- 1 cup water
- Salt to taste

Paste
- 4 red chillies
- 1 teaspoon coriander seeds
- 1 teaspoon red gram dhal
- ¼ teaspoon fenugreek seeds
- ¼ teaspoon peppercorns
- ½ teaspoon asafoetida powder

For Tempering
- 1 teaspoon mustard seeds
- 1 teaspoon cumin seeds
- 1 red chilli, halved
- A few curry leaves

METHOD
1. Roast all the ingredients for the paste. Grind to a fine paste, adding very little water. Set aside.
2. Pressure cook the dhal. Add 1 cup water, tomato, salt and simmer till the tomatoes are done.
3. Add the ground paste and simmer for a couple of minutes.
4. Heat karahi and add all the ingredients for tempering. When the mustard seeds splutter, add to the rasam. Turn off the heat.
5. Add the sour buttermilk. Mix well.
6. Serve hot with rice.

19 | Drumstic Rasam
(Murungaikkai Rasam)

Ingredients

- Lemon-sized tamarind
- 4-5 drumsticks, boiled and the kernel scraped
- One-third cup red gram dhal
- ½ teaspoon turmeric powder
- 1 small bunch coriander leaves,
- Chopped fine
- Salt to taste

Paste

- 4 red chillies
- ½ teaspoon asafoetida powder
- 1 teaspoon coriander seeds
- 1 teaspoon peppercorns
- 1 ½ teaspoons bengal gram dhal

For Tempering

- 1 teaspoon mustard seeds
- 1 teaspoon cumin seeds
- 1 red chilli, halved
- A few curry leaves

METHOD

1. **To make the paste :** Roast all the ingredients for the paste. Grind to a fine paste, adding a little water. Set aside.

2. Pressure cook the dhal. Set aside.

3. Soak the tamarind in 1 cup of water and extract the juice. Add the salt and turmeric powder. Add the scraped drumstick kernel and simmer, till the raw smell of the tamarind completely disappears.

4. Add the ground paste and the cooked dal. Add more water if the rasam is too thick. Simmer till everything blends well.

5. Heat karahi and add all the ingredients for tempering. When the mustard seeds splutter, add to the rasam.

6. Garnish with chopped coriander leaves and serve hot with rice.

Spicy Lentil Rasam
(Poritha Rasam)

20

Ingredients

- ½ cup red gram dhal
- ¼ cup green gram dhal
- 1 tomato
- Juice of 1 lemon
- A pinch of turmeric powder
- A bunch of coriander leaves, chopped fine
- 2 cups water
- salt to taste

Paste

- 1 tablespoon coriander seeds
- 1 teaspoon peppercorns
- 1 teaspoon cumin seeds
- 1 red chilli
- 2 teaspoons black gram dhal
- ½ teaspoon asafoetida powder
- 1 teaspoon mustard seeds
- 1 teaspoon cumin seeds
- 1 red chilli, halved
- A few curry leaves

METHOD

1. Pressure cook the dhals and set aside
2. **To make the paste :** Roast coriander seeds, cumin seeds, peppercorns, red chilli, black gram dhal and asafoetida. Grind to a fine paste using very little water.

3. Heat a pan and add all the ingredients for tempering. When the mustard seeds splutter, add the cooked dhals, chopped tomato, turmeric powder, water and salt, Simmer for a few minutes. Add the ground paste and simmer again for five minutes, till well blended.

4. Add the lemon juice and garnish with chopped coriander leaves.

5. Serve hot with rice.

21

Mysore Rasam

Ingredients
- ½ cup red gram dhal
- 3-4 small tomatoes
- Chopped into large cubes (quartered)
- 3 teaspoons Mysore Rasam powder
- 2 tablespoons jaggery, powdered
- ¼ teaspoon turmeric powder
- 1 small bunch chopped coriander leaves
- Marble-sized tamarind
- Salt to taste

For Tempering
- 1 tablespoon mustard seeds
- 1 teaspoon cumin seeds
- 1 red chilli, halved
- ½ teaspoon asafoetida powder
- A few curry leaves

METHOD
1. Soak the tamarind in 1 cup of water and extract the juice.
2. Pressure cook the red gram dhal and set aside.
3. Heat karahi. Add all the ingredients for tempering. When the mustard seeds splutter, add the chopped tomatoes, tamarind juice. Mysore Rasam powder, salt, turmeric powder and jaggery.
4. Simmer on a low heat for fifteen to twenty minutes, till the raw smell of the tamarind totally disappears.
5. Add the cooked dhal and simmer for another five minutes till everything blends.
6. Garnished with chopped coriander leaves. Serve with hot rice and papadams.

Rasam
(Ordinary Rasam)

22

Ingredients

- 2 tomatoes, cubed
- ½ teaspoon asafoetida powder
- 2 teaspoons Rasam Powder
- 3 tablespoons red gram dhal
- 2 ½ cups water
- Lemon-sized tamarind
- Salt to taste
- Chopped coriander leaves for garnishing

For Tempering

- 1 teaspoon mustard seeds
- ½ teaspoon cumin seeds
- 1 red chilli, halved
- A few curry leaves

METHOD

1. Pressure cook the red gram dhal and set aside.

2. In a pan, add the tomatoes, tamarind, asafoetida powder, rasam powder and salt. Add 1 cup water. Crush everything together, and simmer for about fifteen minutes.

3. Add the cooked dhal and the remaining 1 ½ cups water to the rasam and bring to the boil.

4. Heat a karahi and add all the ingredients for tempering. When the mustard seeds splutter, add to the rasam.

5. Garnish with chopped coriander leaves. Serve hot.

Rasam

Mixed Vegetable Kootu

Mixed Vegetable Kootu

(Avial)

23

Ingredients

- 150 gms ash gourd
- 2 raw plantains
- 2 drumsticks
- 1 potato
- ½ cup shelled peas
- 1 cup sour curds
- ½ teaspoon turmeric powder
- Salt to taste
- A few curry leaves

Paste

- 6-7 green chillies
- 1 teaspoon cumin seeds

METHOD

To make the paste

1. Grind together the green chillies and cumin seeds into a fine paste, adding very little water. Mix curd with the ground paste. Set aside.

2. Peel and chop all the vegetables into 3 inch lengths.

3. Cook the vegetables separately in a heavy-bottomed vessel, adding very little water.

4. Mix all the cooked vegetables together. Add the salt and turmeric powder.

5. Add the paste and heat through, taking care to prevent curdling.

6. Add the curry leaves. Mix well. Do not heat.

7. Serve hot with rice.

24

Beans Poriyal

Ingredients
- ½ kg beans, chopped fine
- Salt to taste

For Tempering
- 1 teaspoon mustard seeds
- 1 teaspoon cumin seeds
- 1 teaspoon black gram dhal
- 1 teaspoon Bengal gram dhal
- 1 red chilli, halved
- ½ teaspoon asafoetida powder
- A few curry leaves

METHOD

1. Heat karahi and add all the ingredients for tempering. When the mustard seeds splutter, add the chopped beans, salt and 2 tablespoons of water.

2. Close the lid and cook on a high heat till the vegetable is tender.

3. Serve hot.

Capsicum Poriyal
(Kudamilagai Poriyal)

25

Ingredients
- ½ kg capsicum, chopped into ½ inch pieces
- 2 tablespoon sour curds
- 2 teaspoons curry powder optional
- Salt to taste

For Tempering
- 1 teaspoon mustard seeds
- 1 teaspoon cumin seeds
- ½ teaspoon asafoetida powder
- A few curry leaves

METHOD

1. Smear the 2 tablespoons curd on the chopped capsicum. Set aside for ten minutes.

2. Heat the karahi, add all the ingredients for tempering. When the mustard seeds splutter, add the chopped capsicum. Add salt and 2 tablespoons water. Simmer covered till done.

3. Sprinkle the curry powder. Fry for a few minutes.

4. Serve hot.

Yam Poriyal
(Chenaikizhangu Poriyal)

26

Ingredients
- ½ kg yam
- ½ teaspoon turmeric powder
- 3 teaspoons curry powder
- 2 green chillies, slit sideways
- Salt to taste

For Tempering
- 1 teaspoon mustard seeds
- 1 teaspoon black gram dhal
- 1 teaspoon Bengal gram dhal
- 1 red chilli, halved
- ½ teaspoon asafoetida powder
- A few curry leaves

METHOD

1. Peel the yam and chop fine. Wash well.

2. Add the salt and turmeric powder and pressure cook, without adding water to the vegetable,

3. Drain in a colander and allow to cool completely.

4. Heat karahi and add all the ingredients for tempering. When the mustard seeds splutter, add the slit green chillies and the cooked vegetable. Stir well.

5. Add the curry powder. Mix well.

6. Serve hot.

· Cabbage Poriyal
(Muttakos Poriyal)

27

Ingredients
- ½ kg cabbage, chopped fine
- ½ cup shelled peas (optional)
- 2 green chillies, slit sideways
- Salt to taste

For Tempering
- 1 teaspoon mustard seeds
- 1 teaspoon cumin seeds
- 1 teaspoon black gram dhal
- 1 teaspoon bengal gram dhal
- 1 red chilli, halved
- ½ teaspoon asafoetida powder
- A few curry leaves

METHOD

1. Heat karahi. Add all the ingredients for tempering.

2. When the mustard seeds splutter, add the chopped green chillies. Stir for a few seconds.

3. Add the chopped cabbage, green peas, salt and 2 tablespoons water. Close with a lid an cooked on a high heat till the vegetables are tender.

4. Serve hot.

(Famous in Tamil Nadu)

28   Plantain Steam Poriyal
(Vazhaithandu Poriyal)

Ingredients
- 1 foot long plantain stem
- ¼ cup green gram dhal
- 2 green chillies, slit sideways.
- 2 teaspoons sugar
- 3 cups thin buttermilk
- Salt to taste

For Tempering
- 1 teaspoon mustard seeds
- 1 teaspoon cumin seeds
- 1 teaspoon black gram dhal
- 1 teaspoon bengal gram dhal
- 1 red chilli, halved
- ½ teaspoon asafoetida powder
- A few curry leaves

METHOD
1. Soak the green gram dal in a cup of water for an hour. Drain and set aside.
2. Chop the plantain stem fine and soak in the buttermilk.
3. Heat karahi and add all the ingredients for tempering. When the mustard seeds splutter, add the green chillies, soaked green gram dhal, chopped plantain stem, salt, sugar and 1 cup water.
4. Cover and simmer on a low heat till the vegetable is done and the water is completely absorbed.
5. Serve hot.

29 | Mashed Potato Poriyal
(Urulaikizhangu Podimas)

Ingredients

- ½ kg potatoes
- 2 green chillies, slit sideways
- 1 inch piece ginger, chopped fine
- 1 bunch coriander leaves, chopped fine
- ½ teaspoon turmeric powder
- Juice of one lemon
- Salt to taste

For Tempering

- 1 teaspoon mustard seeds
- 1 teaspoon black gram dhal
- 1 teaspoon Bengal gram dhal
- 1 red chilli, halved
- ½ teaspoon asafoetida powder
- A few curry leaves

METHOD

1. Pressure cook the potatoes with their jackets; peel, mash and set aside.
2. Heat karahi, add all the ingredients for tempering. When the mustard seeds splutter, add the slit green chillies and ginger, fry for a few seconds.
3. Add the mashed potatoes, salt, turmeric powder. Mix well. Cook for a minute till everything blends well. Turn off the heat.
4. Add the lemon juice. Garnish with chopped coriander leaves.
5. Serve hot.

30 | Beans Dhal Poriyal
(Beans Parupu Usili)

Ingredients
- 1 cup red gram dhal
- 4-5 red chillies
- ¼ teaspoon asafoetida powder
- ½ kg beans, chopped fine
- Salt to taste

For Tempering
- 1 teaspoon mustard seeds
- 1 teaspoon bengal gram dhal
- 1 teaspoon black gram dhal
- 1 red chilli, halved
- ½ teaspoon cumin seeds
- A few curry leaves

METHOD

1. Soak the red gram dhal and the red chillies in water for an hour and grind to a smooth paste, adding salt and asafoetida powder. Set aside.
2. In a heavy pan, cook the beans till tender, adding very little water. Set aside.
3. In the same pan, add all the ingredients for tempering.
4. When the mustard seeds splutter, add the red gram dhal paste and roast on a low heat stirring once in a while, till the mixture is well cooked and crisp (resembling bread crumbs, but not hard)
5. Add the cooked beans and roast for a couple of minutes till everything blends.
6. Serve hot.

Stuffed Brinjal Poriyal
(Sagalay)

31

Ingredients
- ½ kg small-sized brinjals
- Lemon-sized tamarind

Stuffing
- 1 tablespoon coriander seeds
- ¾ tablespoon black gram dhal
- ¾ tablespoon Bengal gram dhal
- 1 teaspoon cumin seeds
- ½ teaspoon asafoetida powder
- 8 red chillies
- Salt to taste

For Tempering
- 1 teaspoon mustard seeds
- 1 teaspoon cumin seeds
- 1 teaspoon black gram dhal
- 1 teaspoon bengal gram dhal
- 1 red chilli, halved
- A few curry leaves

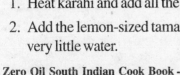

METHOD

To make the stuffing
1. Heat karahi and add all the ingredients for the stuffing.
2. Add the lemon-sized tamarind and grind to a thick paste, adding very little water.

3. **To make the poriyal :** Quarter the brinjals without cutting them through.

4. Fill the quartered brinjals with the stuffing and set aside.

5. Heat the pan and add all the ingredients for tempering. When the mustard seeds splutter, add the stuffed brinjals, salt and a little water. Sprinkle the left over stuffing, if any over the vegetable. Cover and simmer on a low heat, till the brinjals are tender.

6. Remove the lid and roast for a few more minutes without stirring too much. Take care not to break the brinjals.

7. Serve hot with rice.

32

Masala Beans Poriyal

Ingredients
- ½ kg beans, chopped fine
- Salt to taste

Masala
- 3 tablespoons bengal gram dhal
- 1 tablespoon black gram dhal
- 2 tablespoons coriander seeds
- 4 red chillies
- ½ teaspoon asafoetida powder
- Marble-sized tamarind
- Salt to taste

For Tempering
- 1 teaspoon mustard seeds
- 1 teaspoon bengal gram dhal
- 1 teaspoon black gram dhal
- 1 red chilli, halved
- ½ teaspoon asafoetida powder
- 1 teaspoon cumin seeds
- A few curry leaves

METHOD

To make the masala paste

1. Roast bengal garam dhal, black garam dhal, coriander seeds, red chillies and asafoetida. Add the tamarind grind everything to thick paste. Use very little water. Add the salt. Set aside.

2. In a pan, add the chopped beans, salt, a little water and cook on a low heat, till the beans are tender. Set aside.

3. In the same pan add all the ingredients for tempering. When the mustard seeds splutter, add the ground masala paste. Cook on a low heat for five to seven minutes till the mixture is dry and crisp.

4. Add the cooked beans to the masala and cook for another two or three minutes till the masala blends well with the beans.

5. Serve hot with rice.

Colocasia Roast
(Cheppangkizhangu Roast)

33

Ingredients
- 1 kg colocasia
- 1 tablespoon curry powder
- ½ teaspoon turmeric powder
- Salt to taste

For Tempering
- 1 teaspoon mustard seeds
- 1 teaspoon cumin seeds
- 1 teaspoon bengal gram dhal
- 1 teaspoon black gram dhal
- 1 red chilli, halved
- ½ teaspoon asafoetida powder
- A few curry leaves

METHOD

1. Pressure cook the colocasia with the jacket; peel and chop to ½ inch size.

2. Heat the pan. Add all the ingredients for tempering. When the mustard seeds splutter, add the chopped colocasia, salt and turmeric powder.

3. Cook on a low heat for at least half an hour, turning the vegetable every five minutes. Take care not to break the pieces.

4. Roast till golden and sprinkle the curry powder. Mix well.

5. Serve immediately.

34

Plantain Poriyal
(Vazhakkai Poriyal)

Ingredients
- 3 green raw plantains
- ½ teaspoon turmeric powder
- 2 green chillies, slit sideways
- 1 tablespoon curry powder
- Lemon sized tamarind
- Salt to taste

For Tempering
- 1 teaspoon mustard seeds
- 1 teaspoon cumin seeds
- 1 teaspoon black gram dhal
- 1 teaspoon bengal gram dhal
- 1 red chilli halved
- ¼ teaspoon asafoetida powder
- A few curry leaves

METHOD

1. Peel and chop the green plantain to ½ inch size.
2. Soak the tamarind in ¾ cup of water and extract the juice.
3. In a pan, add the chopped plantain, the tamarind juice, turmeric powder and salt and cook covered on a low heat, till the vegetable is tender and dry. Set aside.
4. Heat the pan and add all the ingredients for tempering. When the mustard seeds splutter, add the slit green chillies and the cooked plantain.
5. Add the curry powder and cook for another minute till everything blends well.
6. Serve hot with rice.

Potato Masala
(Potato Paliya)

35

Ingredients
- ½ kg potatoes
- ½ cup boiled peas
- 2 medium sized onions, chopped fine
- 2-3 green chillies, chopped fine
- 1 inch piece ginger, scraped and chopped fine
- ½ teaspoon turmeric powder
- 2 tomatoes, chopped fine
- Salt to taste
- A small bunch coriander leaves, chopped fine
- 1 cup water

For Tempering
- 1 teaspoon mustard seeds
- 1 teaspoon cumin seeds
- 1 teaspoon black gram dhal
- 1 teaspoon bengal gram dhal
- 1 red chilli, halved
- ½ teaspoon asafoetida powder
- A few curry leaves

METHOD
1. Pressure cook the potatoes with their jackets; peel, mash and set aside.
2. Heat the pan. Add all the ingredients for tempering. When the mustard seeds splutter, add the green chillies, ginger, onions and tomatoes. Roast, for a minute or two.
3. Add the salt, turmeric powder and 1 cup water. Close with a lid. Simmer for about five minutes, till the onions are well cooked.
4. Add the mashed potatoes and boiled peas. Cook for two more minutes till everything blends well.
5. Garnish with chopped coriander leaves.
6. Serve hot with masala dosai.

36

Dal Kootu
(Poritha Kootu)

Ingredients
- ¼ cup green gram dhal
- ½ cup beans, chopped fine
- 1 carrot, chopped fine
- 1 potato, peeled and cubed
- ½ cup shelled peas
- ½ teaspoon turmeric powder
- Salt to taste

Paste
- ¾ teaspoon cumin seeds
- 1 teaspoon peppercorns
- 2 red chillies
- ½ teaspoon asafoetida powder

For Tempering
- 1 teaspoon mustard seeds
- ½ teaspoon cumin seeds
- 1 teaspoon black gram dhal
- 1 red chilli, halved
- A few curry leaves

METHOD

1. Pressure cook the green gram dhal. Set aside.
2. To make the paste : Roast the cumin seeds, peppercorns, red chillies and asafoetida powder. Grind to a fine paste, adding very little water.
3. Boil the vegetables with the salt and turmeric powder.
4. Add the cooked dal to the vegetables and simmer for a couple of minutes.
5. Add the ground paste and simmer till everything blends.
6. Heat the pan, add all the ingredients for tempering. When the mustard seeds splutter, add to the kootu.
7. Serve hot, garnished with curry leaves.

37

Tamarind Kootu
(Pulippu Kootu)

Ingredients
- ½ kg ash gourd, peeled and chopped fine
- Marble sized tamarind
- ¼ cup red gram dhal
- ¼ cup Bengal gram dhal
- ½ teaspoon turmeric powder
- Salt to taste

Paste
- 1 ½ teaspoons peppercorns
- 2 teaspoons black gram dhal
- 1 tablespoon bengal gram dhal
- ½ teaspoon asafoetida powder
- 1 tablespoon coriander seeds
- 1 red chilli

For Tempering
- 1 teaspoon mustard seeds
- 1 teaspoon black gram dhal
- 1 red chilli, halved
- A few curry leaves

METHOD
1. Soak the tamarind in 1 cup water and extract the juice. Set aside.

2. Pressure cook together the red gram dhal and the bengal gram dhal. Set aside.

3. Roast all the ingredients for the paste. Grind to a fine paste adding a little water.

4. Heat the pan and add all the ingredients for tempering. When the mustard seeds splutter, add the vegetable, salt, turmeric powder and the tamarind juice.

5. Simmer till the vegetable is tender.

6. Add the cooked dhal and simmer till well blended.

7. Add the ground paste and cook for a few more minutes.

8. Serve hot with rice.

Buttermilk Kootu
(Moru Kootu)

38

Ingredients
- 2 medium sized raw green plantains
- Skinned and chopped fine
- 2 small brinjals, chopped fine
- 1 chow chow, skinned and chopped fine or
- 100 grams snake gourd
- 1 ripe tomato, quartered
- 2 green chillies
- 1 cup fresh curd
- ½ teaspoon turmeric powder
- Salt to taste
- 3 red chillies
- 2 teaspoons coriander seeds
- 1 teaspoon bengal gram dhal
- ½ teaspoon fenugreek seeds

For Tempering
- 1 teaspoon mustard seeds
- A few curry leaves

METHOD
To make the paste
1. Roast all the ingredients for the paste. Add the green chillies and a little water, grind to a fine paste. Add the curd, mix well. Set aside.
2. Heat the pan and add the ingredients for tempering. When the mustard seeds splutter, add the chopped vegetables.
3. Add the salt, turmeric powder and sufficient water and cook covered on a low heat till the vegetables are done.
4. Add the paste and heat through, taking care to prevent curdling.
5. Serve hot with rice.

39

Brinjal Rasavangy
(Kathirikkai Rasavangy)

Ingredients

- 150 gm tender brinjals, quartered
- ½ cup red gram dhal
- 1 small tomato
- 2 green chillies, slit sideways
- ½ teaspoon sambar powder
- 1 tablespoon jaggery, powdered
- Marble-sized tamarind
- Salt to taste

Paste

- 1 ½ tablespoons coriander seeds
- 2 red chillies
- ½ teaspoon asafoetida powder
- 1 teaspoon mustard seeds
- 1 red chilli, halved
- A few curry leaves

METHOD

1. Pressure cook the red gram dhal and set aside.
2. Soak the tamarind in 1 cup water and extract the juice.
3. **To make the Paste :** Roast the coriander seeds, red chillies and asafoetida. Grind to a fine paste. Use very little water.
4. Heat the pan and add the ingredients for tempering. When the

mustard seeds splutter, add the green chillies, chopped tomato and brinjals.

5. Add the salt, turmeric powder, sambar powder, tamarind juice and jaggery and cook on a low heat till the vegetables are done.

6. Add the cooked dhal and the paste. Simmer for a couple of minutes till everything blends well.

7. Garnish with chopped coriander leaves.

8. Serve hot with rice.

40 | Snake Gourd Kootu
(Pudalagai Milagu Kootu)

Ingredients

- 1 medium sized snake gourd (1/2 kg) chopped fine
- ½ teaspoon turmeric powder
- 2 cups water
- Salt to taste

Paste

- 2-3 tablespoons black gram dhal
- 3-4 red chillies
- 3-4 teaspoons cumins seeds
- 1 teaspoon raw rice
- 1 teaspoon mustard seeds
- 1 red chilli, halved
- A few curry leaves

METHOD

1. To make the paste : Roast black gram dhal and red chillies. Grind to a fine paste, along with the cumin seeds and rice, adding a little water.
2. Pressure cook the dhal and set aside.
3. In a closed pan cook the snake gourd in sufficient water with the salt and turmeric powder.
4. When the vegetable is tender, add the dhal. Simmer till everything blends.
5. Add the paste and cook for a couple of minutes. Remove from the heat.
6. Heat the pan and add the ingredients for tempering. When the mustard seeds splutter, add to the milagu kootal
7. Serve hot with rice.

Mashed Amaranth
(Keerai Mashial)

41

Ingredients
- 2 bunches amaranth leaves
- ¼ cup green gram dhal
- Salt to taste

For Tempering
- 1 teaspoon mustard seeds
- 1 teaspoon cumin seeds
- 1 teaspoon black gram dhal
- 1 red chilli, halved
- ½ teaspoon asafoetida powder

METHOD

1. Pressure cook the green gram dhal and set aside.

2. Wash the amaranth leaves and chop fine. Cook the leaves, taking care not to lose the green colour. Blend in a liquidizer (Mixie).

3. Mix the green gram dhal, salt and reheat.

4. Heat the pan and add all the ingredients for tempering. When the mustard seeds splutter, add to the mashed amaranth.

5. Serve hot with rice.

42

Potato Sag

Ingredients

- ½ kg large potatoes
- 4 large onions, diced fine
- 3 teaspoons chilli powder
- 1 ½ teaspoons coriander seeds powder
- 1 bunch coriander leaves, chopped fine
- Lemon-sized tamarind
- Lemon-sized jaggery
- Salt to taste
- A few curry leaves

METHOD

1. Pressure cook the potatoes with their jackets; peel and cut into ½ inch cubes.
2. Soak the tamarind in 1 cup of water and extract the juice and set aside.
3. Heat the pan, add the curry leaves, the chopped onions and roast till golden brown.
4. Add the diced potatoes and roast for two or three minutes.
5. Add the tamarind juice, salt, chilli powder and jaggery and simmer for a couple of minutes.
6. Add the coriander seeds powder and simmer again, till the vegetable is well blended. Turn off the heat.
7. Garnish with the chopped coriander leaves. Serve hot with chapattis.

43

Vegetable Korma

Ingredients
- 1 cup beans
- 1 cup carrots
- 2 potatoes
- 1 big tomato
- ½ cup shelled peas
- ½ bunch coriander leaves for garnishing
- A few bay leaves
- Salt to taste

Paste
- 6-8 green chillies
- 1 small onion
- ½ inch piece ginger
- ½ teaspoon turmeric powder
- 1 small bunch coriander leaves

Masala
- 1 tablespoon aniseeds
- 1 small piece cinnamon
- 6 cloves
- 1 tablespoon poppy seeds

METHOD

1. **To make the paste :** Finely grind the ingredients for the paste, adding a little water.

2. **To make the masala :** Roast dry the ingredients for the masala till they give off a strong aroma. Powder fine.

3. Chop the vegetables fine. Add sufficient water and cook covered. When the vegetables are tender, add the chopped tomato, salt and simmer for a minute or two.

4. Add the paste. Stir well.

5. Sprinkle the masala. Mix well.

6. Heat karahi, roast the bay leaves and add to the korma.

7. Serve hot with phulkas. It is also an excellent accompaniment to idlis and dosas.

Mixed Vegetable Sagu
(Sagu)

44

Ingredients
- 1 cup mixed vegetables
  (chow chow, cabbage and beans)
- 2 carrots
- 1 potato
- ¼ kg shelled peas
- 1 onion, chopped fine
- ½ teaspoon turmeric powder
- 1 bunch coriander leaves for garnishing
- Salt to taste

Paste
- 4-5 green chillies
- 1 tablespoon roasted gram dhal
- ¼ teaspoon peppercorns
- 3 teaspoons coriander seeds powder
- 1 teaspoon cumin seeds
- 1 small stick cinnamon
- 2-3 cloves

For Tempering
- 1 teaspoon mustard seeds
- 1 red chilli, halved
- 1 teaspoon black gram dhal
- ½ teaspoon asafoetida powder
- A few curry leaves

METHOD

1. Chop the mixed vegetables, carrots and potato to ½ inch size.

2. Grind all the ingredients for the paste in a raw state and set aside. Use very little water.

3. Heat the pan and add all the ingredients for tempering. When the mustard seeds splutter, add the chopped onion and sauté for a couple of minutes.

4. Add the chopped vegetables, peas, salt, turmeric powder and sufficient water. Simmer till the vegetables are tender.

5. Add the ground paste and simmer for a couple of minutes.

6. Garnish with chopped coriander leaves.

7. Serve hot with phulkas.

45

Potato Sukke

Ingredients

- 750 gms potatoes
- 2 tablespoons grated jaggery
- ½ teaspoon turmeric powder
- Lemon sized tamarind
- Salt to taste

Paste

- 4-6 red chillies
- ½ teaspoon fenugreek seeds
- 3 teaspoons black gram dhal
- 4 teaspoons coriander seeds

For Tempering

- 1 teaspoon mustard seeds
- A few curry leaves

METHOD

1. Peel and chop the potatoes to ½ inch pieces. Set aside.

2. **To make the paste :** Heat the pan and roast the red chillies. Set aside.

3. Roast the fenugreek seeds, black gram dhal and coriander seeds.

4. In a liquidizer, grind tamarind and the red chillies to a fine paste, adding a little water. When almost smooth, add the coriander seeds, fenugreek seeds and black gram dhal and grind them coarsely.

5. Heat pan and add the mustard seeds and curry leaves. When the mustard seeds splutter, add the potatoes, turmeric powder, salt and sufficient water to cover the potatoes. Close with a lid and simmer till the potatoes are tender.

6. Add the ground paste and the powdered jaggery. Add more water if the vegetable is too dry. Simmer till everything blends. Remove from heat.

7. Serve hot with phulkas or as a side dish to rice.

Vegetable Medley
(Thakkali-Vellarikkai Carrot Kosumalli)

46

Ingredients
- 1 carrot, peeled and chopped fine
- 1 cucumber, peeled and chopped fine
- 1 tomato, chopped fine
- 1 small bunch coriander leaves, chopped fine
- 2 tablespoons lemon juice
- Salt to taste

For Tempering
- 1 teaspoon mustard seeds
- 1 teaspoon cumin seeds
- 1 teaspoon black gram dhal
- 1 red chilli, halved
- ½ teaspoon asafoetida powder
- A few curry leaves

METHOD

1. Mix all the vegetables. Add the salt.
2. Heat pan. Add all the ingredients for tempering.
3. When the mustards seeds splutter, add to the vegetables.
4. Add the lemon juice and mix well.
5. Serve cold or at room temperature.

47 Green Cucumber Salad
(Vellarikkai Kosumalli)

Ingredients
- 2 tablespoons green gram dhal
- 1 large cucumber, skinned and chopped fine
- 1 green chilli, chopped fine
- 1 small bunch coriander leaves, chopped fine
- 1 tablespoon lemon juice
- Salt to taste

For Tempering
- 1 teaspoon mustard seeds
- 1 teaspoon cumin seeds
- 1 teaspoon black gram dhal
- 1 teaspoon bengal gram dhal
- ½ teaspoon asafoetida powder
- 1 red chilli, halved
- A few curry leaves

METHOD

1. Soak the green gram dhal in a cup of water for an hour.

2. Mix the chopped cucumber, green chilli, coriander leaves, salt and lemon juice.

3. Add the soaked green gram dhal and mix well.

4. Heat the pan and add all the ingredients for tempering. When the mustard seeds splutter, add to the salad, Mix well.

5. Serve chilled or at room temperature.

Green Cucumber Salad

Mixed Vegetable Curd Salad

(Famous in Karnataka)

48 | Mixed Vegetable Curd Salad
(Vellarikkai Thakkali Vengaya Pachadi)

Ingredients

- 1 medium sized cucumber, peeled and chopped fine
- 1 ripe tomato, chopped fine
- 1 medium sized onion, chopped fine
- 1-2 green chillies, chopped fine
- 1 small bunch of coriander leaves, chopped fine
- 2 cups fresh curd
- Salt to taste

For Tempering

- 1 teaspoon mustard seeds
- 1 teaspoon cumin seeds
- 1 teaspoon black gram dhal
- 1 teaspoon bengal gram dhal
- ½ teaspoon asafoetida powder
- 1 red chilli, halved
- A few curry leaves

METHOD

1. In a bowl, mix the cucumber, tomato, onions, green chillies, coriander leaves, and salt with the curd.
2. Heat the pan and add all the ingredients for tempering. When the mustard seeds splutter, add to the salad.
3. Mix well. Garnish with chopped coriander leaves.
4. Serve cold or at room temperature.

49   Mango Curd Salad
(Mangai Pachadi)

Ingredients
- 1 small raw mango, skinned and chopped fine
- 4 green chillies
- 1 teaspoon cumin seeds
- 2 cups fresh curd
- A bunch of coriander leaves
- Salt to taste

For Tempering
- 1 teaspoon mustard seeds
- 1 teaspoon cumin seeds
- ¼ teaspoon asafoetida powder
- 1 red chilli, halved
- A few curry leaves

METHOD

1. Grind the mango, green chillies, and cumin seeds into a fine paste in a liquidizer, using a little water.

2. In a serving, dish mix the curd with the ground paste. Add salt.

3. Heat the pan and add all the ingredients for tempering. When the mustard seeds splutter, add to the salad.

4. Garnish with coriander leaves and serve cold or at room temperature.

50 Ladies' Fingers Curd Salad
(Vendakkai Thair Pachadi)

Ingredients
- ¼ kg lady's finger
- 1 ½ cups well mixed fresh curd
- Salt to taste

For Tempering
- 1 teaspoon mustard seeds
- 1 teaspoon cumin seeds
- 1 teaspoon black gram dhal
- 1 teaspoon Bengal gram dhal
- 1 red chilli, halved
- ¼ teaspoon asafoetida powder
- A few curry leaves

METHOD

1. Stem and chop finely lady's finger.
2. Heat the pan. Add all the ingredients for tempering.
3. When the mustard seeds splutter, add the ladies' fingers. Cook on a low heat till the vegetable is tender.
4. Add the salt and cook for a minute. Allow the vegetable is tender.
5. Add the well-mixed curds and blend well.
6. Serve cold or at room temperature.

51

Spinach Stew
(Palakoora Pulusu)

Ingredients
- 1 bunch spinach leaves
- tamarind, the size of a big lemon
- 2 ripe tomatoes
- 2 small onions
- 1 tbsp sugar
- ½ tbsp chilli powder
- 1 tsp peeled black gram
- 1 tbsp cumin seeds
- 1 tbsp mustard
- A pinch asafoetida
- Salt to taste

METHOD

1. Clean spinach leaves. Chop into small pieces and boil.

2. Add water to tamarind and squeeze out a small bowl of tamarind juice.

3. Chop onions and tomatoes into medium sized pieces.

4. Put spinach leaves, tamarind juice, onions and tomatoes into a frying pan, add half a glass of water and cook. Add chilli powder, sugar and salt. Cook until thick.

5. Heat the frying plan. Roast black gram cumin seeds, mustard and asafoetida. Add this seasoning to the stew.

(Famous in Andhra Pradesh)

52

Fenugreek Yoghurt Stew
(Menthi Majjiga)

Ingredients
- 1½ yoghurt (1 day sour)
- Turmeric, a pinch
- Coriander leaves, a stem
- ½ tsp. mustard
- ½ tsp. cumin seeds
- ½ tsp. peeled black gram
- A pinch asafoetida
- 2 green chillies
- ½ red chilli
- Salt to taste

METHOD
1. Beat yoghurt
2. Chop green chillies finely. Pluck coriander. Add salt and turmeric to the yoghurt.
3. Roast mustad, cumin seeds, black gram, asafoetida and red chilli. Season.

53   Gram flour Yoghurt Stew
(Majjiga Pulusu)

Ingredients

- 2 cups a day old yoghurt
- a pinch - turmeric
- 1 stem - curry leaves
- 1 tsp chilli powder
- 1 small piece ginger
- 2 green chillies
- ½ tsp mustard
- ½ tsp. cumin seeds
- A pinch – asafoetida
- 200 gms pumpkin (or any other vegetable)
- 1 tbsp gram flour
- Salt to taste

METHOD

1. Boil vegetables until firm and cooked.
2. Beat the yoghurt. Mix gram flour in it, without lumps.
3. Add turmeric, salt, chilli powder, curry leaves and a cup of water to the yoghurt. Add vegetables.
4. Grind green chillies and ginger. Add to yoghurt.
5. Cook. Allow it to thicken, stirring it all the while, to stop it from boiling over. Simmer on low heat. Remove after it is well blended.
6. Roast mustard, cumin seeds and asafoetida. Season.

54

Cabbage Stew
(Cabbage Kootu)

Ingredients

- 1 cup tur dal
- 200 gms cabbage
- 50 gms french beans
- 1 tomato, ripe
- 1 Drumstick
- 1 tsp thick tamarind juice
- 1 tsp sugar
- 1 tsp chilli powder
- ½ tsp asafoetida
- ½ tsp mustard seeds
- 1 tbsp dhaniya seeds
- 6 Pepper seeds
- Salt to taste

METHOD

1. Boil dal
2. Chop vegetables into small pieces. Boil.
3. Mix both, with chilli powder, salt, asafoetida, sugar and tamarind juice.
4. Heat oil. Fry black gram and mustard seeds.
5. Grind dhaniya seeds and pepper seeds.
6. Add both masalas to the kootu, cook for 5 minutes on low heat.

55 Green Gram Stew
(Pesarapappu Kootu)

Ingredients

- ½ cup moong dhal, yellow, broken
- 1 – potato, big
- 1 – drumstick
- 200 gms lauki
- 1 inch piece coconut
- ½ ts chilli powder
- 2 green chillies
- 1 stem curry leaves
- ½ tsp asafoetida
- Salt to taste

For Masala

- ½ tsp urad dhal
- ½ tsp mustard seeds
- ½ tsp jeera
- ½ tsp pepper powder

METHOD

1. Clean and boil the dhal
2. Chop vegetables into small pieces and boil.
3. Grind coconut and green chillies together.
4. Mix all and cook on low heat, for 5 minutes. Add salt asafoetida and chilli powder.
5. Roast masala and add to the kootu.

Fenugreek Stew
(Menthi Pulusu)

56

Ingredients
- ½ tsp. - fenugreek seeds
- 1 tomato, ripe
- 1 drumstick
- 2 onions (small)
- 1 katori tamarind juice
- ½ tsp peeled black gram
- ½ tsp cumin seeds
- ½ tsp jaggery
- 1 stem curry leaves
- Salt to taste

METHOD
1. Chop vegetables.
2. Roast methi seeds.
3. Add tamarind juice, ½ cup water, jaggery and salt. Boil for 5 minutes.
4. Roast black gram, cumin seeds and curry leaves. Season.

57   Gongura Pulusu
(Sorrel Stew)

Ingredients

- Sorrel with sour leaves and red stems – 1 medium sized bunch
- Onions-1
- Mustard – ½ tsp
- Peeled black gram – ½ tsp Asafoetida – a pinch
- Bengal gram – 1/3 cup
- Chilli powder – 2 tsp
- Green chillies – 2
- Salt to taste

METHOD

1. Pluck the sorrel leaves. Clean well. Add ½ a glass of water and cook.

2. Chop the onions into medium sized pieces. Chop green chillies. Add to the sorrel. Add chilli powder and salt.

3. Boil bengal gram in one glass of water. Add to the sorrel.Stir.Cook until thick.

4. Roast mustard, black gram and asafoetida. Season.

58 Mixed Vegetable Stew
(Mukkala Pulusu)

Ingredients

- Recommended vegetables
- Drumstick – 1
- Sweet potato – 1
- Red Pumpkin – ¼
- Ladies finger – 4
- Tamarind, the size of big lemon
- Chilli powder – 2 tbsp
- Turmeric – a pinch
- Asafoetida – a pinch
- Curry leaves – a stem
- Cumin seeds – ½ tsp
- Mustard – 1/2tsp
- Salt to taste

METHOD

1. Soak tamarind in water. Extract a cup of juice.
2. Chop vegetables to make a full cup of vegetables.
3. Boil vegetables until cooked, but not too soft. But don't add ladies finger.
4. Add the vegetable pieces to the tamarind juice, add one cup of water, chilli powder, turmeric, curry leaves, salt and jaggery. Cook if you use pumpkin mashes, lightly. Cook until thick.
5. Roast cumin seeds, asafoetida and mustard. Season.

59

Roast Brinjal Stew
(Pacchi Brinjal Stew)

Ingredients

- 1 fresh and round brinjal
- Tamarind, the size of a lemon
- A pinch – turmeric
- A pinch – asafoetida
- 1 tsp sugar
- ½ tsp mustard
- ½ tsp black gram
- 2 green chillies
- 1 stem coriander leaves
- Salt to taste

METHOD

1. Roast the brinjal, turning it on all four sides. When soft and when the skin turns black and cracky, remove. Cool in water. Peel skin. Cut it carefully with a knife, checking to see if there are worms. If not, mash lightly.

2. Chop green chillies finely.

3. Add green chillies, salt, turmeric and sugar to the brinjal.

4. Soak tamarind – extract half a cup of thin tamarind juice. Add to brinjal. Mix.

5. Roast mustard, black gram, asafoetida and coriander leaves. Season.

Greenberry Dal
(Vagkkai Parpu)

60

Ingredients
- Moong dhal — ½ cup
- Vagkkai — 50 gms
- Green Chillies — 2
- Chilli powder — 1 tsp

For masala
- Black gram — ½ tsp
- Mustard seeds — ½ tsp
- Cumin seeds — ½ tsp
- Curry leaves — 1 stem
- A pinch of asafoetida

METHOD

1. Boil moong dhal. Chop green chillies.

2. Cut vagkkai to remove seeds and add to dhal. Add salt , chilli powder and green chillies. Cook till thick.

3. Roast masala and season.

61

Lemon Dal
(Nimmakai Pappu)

Ingredients

- Tur gram — ½ cup
- A big lemon — ½
- Turmeric — a pinch
- Mango ginger — a big piece
- Green chillies — 2
- Curry leaves — 1 stem
- Peeled black gram — ½ tsp
- Mustard — ½ tsp
- Red Chilli — 1
- Asafoetida — a pinch
- Salt to taste

METHOD

1. Extract lemon juice.
2. Peel the mango ginger and chop finely. Chop the green chillies finely. Clean and pluck curry leaves.
3. Boil the tur gram well.
4. Add salt and turmeric and cook. Remove when thick. Add lemon juice, green chillies, curry leaves and mango ginger.
5. Break red chilli into pieces. Roast black gram, mustard, red chilli and asafoetida.

   Add to dal as seasoning.

Sorrel Dal
(Gangura Pappu)

62

Ingredients

- Tur gram - ½ cup
- Chilli powder — 1 tsp
- Sorrel leaves — ½ bunch
- Peeled black gram — 1 tsp
- Mustard seeds — 1 tsp
- Green chillies — 2
- Small Onions — 2
- Asafoetida — a pinch
- Salt to taste

METHOD

1. Boil the tur gram.

2. Chop green chillies finely. Chop onions.

3. Pour tur gram into a frying pan. Add sorrel leaves, chillies and onions. Add half a glass of water and cook until leaves and onions soften.

4. Add salt and chilli powder. Stir. Cook until thick.

5. Roast mustard, black gram and asafoetida –add to the dhal.

63 | Tamarind Leaf Dhal
(Chinta Chiguru Pappu)

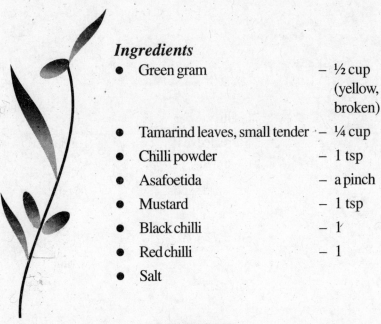

Ingredients

- Green gram — ½ cup (yellow, broken)
- Tamarind leaves, small tender — ¼ cup
- Chilli powder — 1 tsp
- Asafoetida — a pinch
- Mustard — 1 tsp
- Black chilli — 1
- Red chilli — 1
- Salt

METHOD

1. Clean tamarind leaves.
2. Add a cup of water and boil both leaves and green gram together.
3. Break the red chilli into small pieces. Roast mustard, black gram and red chilli.
4. Add dhal and leaves to the seasoning and cook on a low heat. Add salt, chilli powder and asafoetida. Remove when thick.

Colocasia Leaf Dhal
(Chamadumpaku Pappu)

64

Ingredients

- Green gram peeled, broken   – ½cup
- Colocassia leaves   – 3 big
- Chilli powder   – 1tsp
- Curry leaves   – 1stem
- Green chilli   – 1
- Salt to taste

METHOD

1. Put one leaf on another, roll together, and chop finely to make long pieces.

2. Boil green gram and leaves in a cup of water.

3. Chop green chilli.

4. Add salt, chilli powder and green chillies. Cook until thick.

5. Roast mustard, cumin seeds and curry leaves, add as seasoning.

65 | Andhra Cucumber Dhal
(Dosakai Pappu)

Ingredients

- Tur gram — ½ cup
- Andhra cucumber — 1 small
- Chilli powder — 1 tbsp
- Red chilli — 1
- Tamarind juice — 2 tbsp
- Mustard — ½ tsp
- Peeled black gram — ½ tsp
- Turmeric — a pinch
- Asafoetida — a pinch
- Salt to taste

METHOD

1. Boil tur gram until soft.

2. Peel cucumber, check to see if it is sour, if not, cut into medium sized pieces.

3. Break red chilli into small pieces. Roast red chilli, mustard, black gram asafetida and turmeric.

4. Add cucumber, tamarind juice and half cup water, cook on low heat until pieces are ready. Add dhal and stir. Add salt and chilli powder. Stir.

<table>
<tr><td>

66

</td><td>

Fenugreek Dhal
(Menthi Aku Pappu)

</td></tr>
</table>

Ingredients

- Yellow peeled green gram   – ½ cup
- Fenugreek leaves   – ¼ bunch
- Green chilli   – 1
- Chilli powder   – ½ tsp
- Cumin seeds   – ½ tsp
- Mustard   – ½ tsp
- Salt to taste

METHOD

1. Clean the gram.

2. Pluck fenugreek leaves and clean.

3. Boil gram and fenugreek leaves together. Simmer until thick. Add salt and chilli powder.

   Roast cumin seeds, mustard and green chilli and add to the dhal.

67

Mango Dhal
(Mamidikai Pappu)

Ingredients

Small, sour, raw manoges	– 2
Chilli powder	– 1tbsp
Mustard seeds	– 1 tsp
Cumin	– ½
Tur gram	– 1cup
Peeled black gram	– ½ tsp
Curry leaves	– 1 pinch
Asafoetida	– a pinch
Turmeric	– a pinch
Salt to taste	
Onion	– 1

METHOD

1. Peel mangoes. Cut and remove the shells. Chop the mango flesh into small pieces. Chop onion

2. Boil tur gram and keep aside.

3. Roast mustard, cumin seeds, turmeric, black gram, curry leaves and asafoetida.

4. Add mango pieces, onion pieces and salt. Add a glass of water and cook on low heat until the mango pieces are soft.

5. Add tur gram and stir.

6. Add chilli powder. Stir. Cook until thick.

Drumstick Curry
(Mulakkada Koora)

68

Ingredients

- Drumsticks, fleshy and tender – 4
- Mustard seeds – 1 tbsp
- Cumin seeds – 1 tbsp
- Dry bengal gram – 1 tbsp
- Gram flour – 2 tbsp
- Chilli powder – tbsp
- Jaggery – the size of a small lemon
- Curry leaves – 1 sprig
- Salt to taste

METHOD

1. Cut the drumsticks into quarters. Add salt and boil. Cool.

2. Open the sticks and remove the flesh inside.

3. Roast mustard, cumin seeds, dry bengal gram and curry leaves. Add gram flour. Roast. Add drumstick flesh, chilli powder and jaggery. Beat to mix. Stir. Remove when thick.

69

Bittergourd Curry
(Kakarkai Koora)

Ingredients

- Bittergourd — 300 gms
- Gram flour — 2 tbsp
- Peeled, broken black gram - ½ tbsp
- Mustard - ½ tsp
- Tamarind — the size of a lemon
- Cumin seeds - ½ tsp
- Jaggery — the size of a big lemon
- Chilli powder — 1 tbsp
- Turmeric - a pinch
- Asafoetida — pinch
- Curry leaves — 1 sprig
- Salt to taste

METHOD

1. Chop the bittergourd in circles. Remove seeds. Boil and cool.

2. Soak tamarind in water and extract 2 tbsp. Of thick tamarind juice.

3. Roast black gram, cumin seeds, mustard turmeric and asafoetida. Add bittergourd and curry leaves. Roast on low heat till golden brown.

4. Add tamarind juice, chilli powder, salt and jaggery. Stir.

5. Sprinkle gram flour on it. Keep on low heat till almost crisp.

(Famous in Andhra Pradesh)

Banana Stem Curry
(Arati Doota Koora)

70

Ingredients

- Banana stem
- Tamarind juice   – 1 tbsp
- Chilli powder   – 1 tbsp
- Urad dhal   – ½ tsp
- Mustard seeds   – 1 tbsp
- Asafoetida   – ½ tsp
- Green chillies   – 2
- Curry leaves   – 1 stem
- A pinch of haldi
- Salt to taste

METHOD

1. Pluck the small white flowers. Remove the long stem inside each flower.

2. Cut the white flowers, grind with salt and turmeric . Pressure cook till soft. Squeeze out the water.

3. Chop green chillies. Wet mustard powder. Add these, with tamarind juice, chilli powder and salt to the flower.

4. Roast black gram, mustared seeds, channa dhal, curry leaves, chillies and asafoetida. Add to the curry. Cook on low heat till dry.

Banana Flower Curry
(Arati Puvva Koora)

71

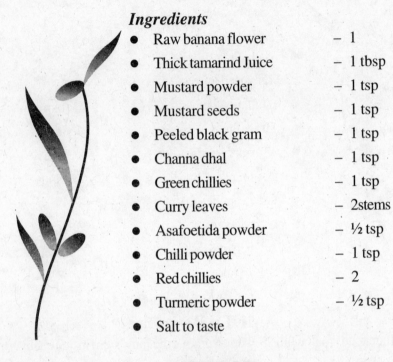

Ingredients

• Raw banana flower	– 1
• Thick tamarind Juice	– 1 tbsp
• Mustard powder	– 1 tsp
• Mustard seeds	– 1 tsp
• Peeled black gram	– 1 tsp
• Channa dhal	– 1 tsp
• Green chillies	– 1 tsp
• Curry leaves	– 2 stems
• Asafoetida powder	– ½ tsp
• Chilli powder	– 1 tsp
• Red chillies	– 2
• Turmeric powder	– ½ tsp
• Salt to taste	

METHOD

1. Pluck the small white flowers. Remove the long stem inside each flowers.

2. Cut the white flowers, grind with salt and turmeric. Pressure cook till soft. Squeeze out the water.

3. Chop green chillies. Wet mustard powder. Add these, with tamarind juice, chilli powder and salt to the flower.

4. Roast black gram, mustard seeds, channa dhal, curry leaves, chillies and asafoetida. Add to the curry. Cook on a low heat till dry.

Snakegourd In Youghurt
(Pottlakai Perugu Pacchadi)

72

Ingredients

•	Tender snakegourd	- 300gms
•	Green chillies	– 3
•	Chilli powder	- 1½ tsp
•	Fresh, thick yoghurt	- 1½cup
•	Mustard	- ½ tsp
•	Cumin seeds	- ½ tsp
•	Dry bengal gram	- ½ tsp
•	Curry leaves	- 1 Sprig
•	Turmeric	– 1pinch
•	Salt	– 1 tbsp

METHOD

1. Chop snakegourd in circles. Remove hard seeds. Sprinkle salt on the snakegourd, mix well. Keep aside for 5 minutes.

2. Squeeze well to drain out the salt water.

3. Roast cumin seeds, green chillies, mustard and dry bengal gram.

4. Add snakegourd, turmeric and chilli powder. Cook till soft. Cool well.

5. Add a pinch of salt to the yoghurt. Add curry leaves. Add snake gourd curry. Mix.

(Famous in Andhra Pradesh)

| **73** | # Board Beans Curry
(Chikkudukai Koora) |

Ingredients

● Broad beans	– 300gms
● Peeled black gram	– ½ tsp
● Mustard	– ½ tsp
● Gram flour	– 1 tbsp
● Tamarind juice	– 2 tbsp
● Sugar	– 2 tbsp
● Chilli powder	– 1 tsp

METHOD

1. Chop beans into 1 inch pieces. Boil with salt.

2. Roast black gram and mustard. Add beans to the frying pan.

3. Add gram flour, tamarind juice, sugar and chilli powder. Fry till almost dry. Stir.

Ribbed Gourd Curry
(Beerakai Koora)

74

Ingredients

- Tur gram   – ½ cup
- Ribbed gourd   – 400 gms
- Chilli powder   – 1 tsp
- Curry leaves   – 1 stem
- Mustard   – ½ tsp
- Bengal gram   – ½ tsp
- Red chilli   – 1

METHOD

1. Peel gourd. Grind skin lightly in a dry grinder. Boil in half cup water. Strain out the water.

2. Boil tur gram until cooked but not too soft.

3. Break red chilli into small pieces. Add bengal gram and mustard. Roast.

4. Squeeze out the water from gourd skin, and add to the frying pan. Add tur gram and salt. Add curry leaves and chilli powder. Roast on low heat until dry.

75 | Andhra Cucumber Curry
(Dosakai Koora)

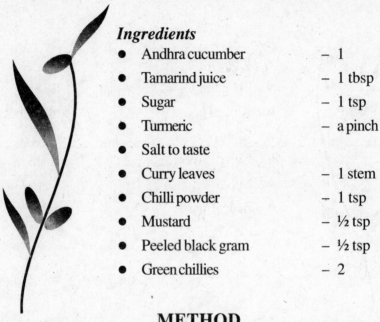

Ingredients

- Andhra cucumber — 1
- Tamarind juice — 1 tbsp
- Sugar — 1 tsp
- Turmeric — a pinch
- Salt to taste
- Curry leaves — 1 stem
- Chilli powder — 1 tsp
- Mustard — ½ tsp
- Peeled black gram — ½ tsp
- Green chillies — 2

METHOD

1. Peel cucumber. Cut into medium-sized pieces. Check to see if the pieces – or the seeds – are sour. If not, then proceed. Chop green chilies. Pluck curry leaves from stem.

2. Roast mustard, black gram, green chillies and curry leaves.

3. Add cucumber, salt, chilli powder, tamarind, turmeric. When cooked, sprinkle sugar. Cook for two more minutes.

Stuffed Brinjal Andhra Curry
(Gutthi Vankai Koora)

76

Ingredients
- Slender brinjal — 300 gms
- Onion — 2
- Tamarind

For Masala
- Bengal gram — 4 tbsp
- Fengureek — 1 tsp
- Coriander seeds — 1 tbsp
- Mustard — 1 tsp
- Red chillies — 6

For Curry
- Salt to taste

METHOD

1. Roast masala and grind.

2. Chop the onion. Add onion and tamarind to the masala, grind again.

3. Slit the short, gourd lengthways into four, without cutting off the crown.

4. Stuff them with masala. Roast on low heat, turning them carefully so that the masala does not fall out. Add salt. Remove when cooked.

Stuffed Ladyfinger Curry
(Bendakai Gutthi Koora)

Ingredients

- Ladies' fingers   – 300gms
- Cumin seeds   – 4 tbsp
- Chilli powder   – 3 tbsp
- Salt to taste

METHOD

1. Make one inch slit lengthways, in the center of the lady fingers.

2. Grind together the cumin seeds, chilli powder and salt, after adding a few drops of water.

3. Stuff the lady fingers with this mixture, and cook on low heat until cooked.

Gram Curry
(Pattholi)

Ingredients

- broken peeled green gram — 1 cup
- green chillies — 2
- tsp cumin seeds — 1½ tsp
- Bengal gram — ½ tsp
- mustard — ½ tsp
- stem curry leaves — 1
- a pinch asafoetida
- chilli powder — 1 tsp
- Salt to taste

METHOD

1. Soak the green gram for 3 hours. Grind with ¼ cup water. Add green chillies, 1 tsp cumin seeds and salt and grind again.

2. Roast bengal gram, mustard, ½ tsp cumin seeds, curry leaves and asafoetida. Add green gram mixture to the frying pan. Cook on low heat. Keep stirring, so that it does not get burnt. Add chilli powder. Stir. Remove when dry.

3. This curry is an unusual accompaniment with chapatis or rice.

79	# Cluster Beans Curry
	(Gori Chikkudukai Koora)

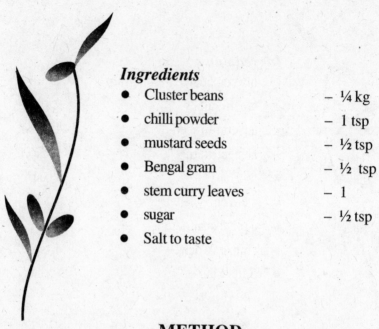

Ingredients

- Cluster beans — ¼ kg
- chilli powder — 1 tsp
- mustard seeds — ½ tsp
- Bengal gram — ½ tsp
- stem curry leaves — 1
- sugar — ½ tsp
- Salt to taste

METHOD

1. Chop beans into small pieces. Boil with salt and a little water.

2. Roast mustard, bengal gram and curry leaves. Add beans and chilli powder stir.

3. Sprinkle sugar. Stir until dry.

Ingredients
- ½ kg raw rice
- ½ tsp yeast
- Salt to taste
- 3 tsp sugar
- ½ cup cooked rice

METHOD

1. Soak rice for 4 hrs and drain it.Grind this in a mixie.

2. Put yeast, salt, sugar in boiled water and keep it for ½ an hr. Then add this to the grinded mixture.

3. Keep the mixture for 8 hrs for fermentation.

4. When it is ready to use, spread the mixture in a non-sticky pan . See that the mixture is spread so that the edge of the appam will be lace structured.

5. Close the pan with the lid and heat it for 2 mts. In the preparation of appam, it is only required to cook on one side. Serve hot with potato curry

(Famous in Tamil Nadu)

| 81 |

Curd Rice
(Thair Sadam)

Ingredients
- 1 cup raw rice
- 1 small raw mango,
- Skinned and chopped fine (optional)
- 1 cucumber, skinned and chopped fine
- 2 green chillies, chopped fine
- 1-inch piece ginger, chopped fine
- 2 cups fresh curd (skim milk)
- ½ cup fresh skim milk
- 1 bunch coriander leaves, chopped fine
- 1 carrot, skinned and grated for garnishing
- Salt to taste

For Tempering
- 1 teaspoon mustard seeds
- 2 teaspoons black gram dhal
- 2 teaspoons bengal gram dhal
- 1 red chilli, halved
- ½ teaspoon asafoetida powder
- A few curry leaves

METHOD
1. Pressure cook the rice.
2. Mash the rice. Add the chopped mango, cucumber and salt.
3. Heat the pan and add all the ingredients for tempering. When the mustard seeds splutter, add to the rice.
4. Add the chopped green chillies, ginger and part of the chopped coriander leaves.. Mix well. Add the curds and milk. Mix thoroughly.
5. Transfer to a serving bowl. Garnish with the grated carrot and coriander leaves.
6. Serve at room temperature or chill slightly in a refrigerator.

Chutney Powder
(Chutney Podi)

82

Ingredients
- ½ cup bengal gram dhal
- ½ cup black gram dhal
- 10-12 red chillies
- ½ teaspoon asafoetida powder
- 1 tablespoon jaggery, powdered
- Marble-sized tamarind
- A few curry leaves
- Salt to taste

METHOD

1. Roast dry the bengal gram dhal, black gram dhal.
2. Roast the red chillies and the asafoetida powder.
3. Mix all the ingredients together and powder fine. Add salt.
4. Serve with hot rice.

83	# Tomato Rice ## (Thakkali Sadam)

Ingredients
- 1 cup long grained rice
- 4 large tomatoes
- 2-3 medium onions, chopped fine
- 2 green chillies, chopped fine
- ½ teaspoon turmeric powder
- Salt to taste

Masala
- 6 red chillies
- 2 teaspoons coriander seeds
- 3 teaspoons bengal gram dhal
- 1 teaspoon black gram dhal
- ¼ teaspoon fenugreek seeds
- ½ teaspoon asafoetida powder

For Tempering
- 1 teaspoon mustard seeds
- A few curry leaves

METHOD

1. Chop the tomatoes and blend in a liquidizer (Mixie). Strain the juice. Set aside.
2. Roast all the ingredients for the masala. Powder fine. Set aside.
3. Pressure cook the rice and spread on a platter to cool.
4. In a pan add the tomato juice, salt and turmeric powder and simmer, till it thickens. Add the ground masala powder and mix well. Set aside.
5. Heat karahi and add all the ingredients for tempering. When the mustard seeds splutter, add chopped green chillies, onions and roast for a few minutes till they are golden. Add the rice and the cooked tomato concentrate. Mix well.
6. Serve hot.

84

Tamarind Rice
(Pullidarrai)

Ingredients
To make the tamarind chutney
(Pullikaichal)

- 1 big lump tamarind (size of an orange)
- ½ teaspoon turmeric powder
- 2 tablespoons jaggery, powdered
- Salt to taste

Masala

- ½ cup coriander seeds,
- 8 red chillies
- ½ teaspoon asafoetida powder
- 1 teaspoon peppercorns
- 1 teaspoon cumin seeds
- 1 teaspoon fenugreek seeds
- ½ teaspoon mustard seeds
- 1 tablespoon bengal gram dhal
- 1 tablespoon black gram dhal
- A few curry leaves

- Garnishing Powder
- ½ cup white sesame seed

For Tempering

- 2 teaspoon mustard seeds
- 1 tablespoon Bengal gram dhal
- 10 red chillies
- A few curry leaves

METHOD

1. Soak the tamarind in 3 cups water and extract the juice. Set aside.
2. Roast all the ingredients for the masala and powder fine. Set aside.
3. Roast dry the sesame seeds. Powder fine and set aside the garnishing powder.
4. Heat the pan, add the red chillies and roast till dark brown.
5. Add the remaining ingredients for tempering. When the mustard seeds splutter, add the tamarind juice, salt, turmeric powder and jaggery.
6. Simmer on a low heat, till everything thickens to almost a jam consistency.
7. Add the powdered masala. Mix well.
8. Add 2 tablespoons of the garnishing powder. Blend well. Set aside the remaining powder for garnishing the rice.

85

Mango Rice
(Mangai Ogaray)

Ingredients
- 1 cup long-grained rice
- 1 ½ cups grated raw mango
- Salt to taste

Masala
- 1 ½ teaspoons mustard seeds
- ½ teaspoon asafoetida powder
- 6 red chillies
- ½ teaspoon turmeric powder

For Tempering
- 1 teaspoon mustard seeds
- 1 tablespoon bengal gram dhal
- 1 red chilli, halved
- A few curry leaves

METHOD

1. Cook the rice and set aside.
2. Grind the ingredients for the masala to a fine paste, adding ½ the grated mango.
3. Heat the pan, add all the ingredients for tempering. When the mustard seeds splutter, add the bengal gram dhal and roast till it turns golden, add the remaining grated mango. Cook for a few minutes on a medium heat till the mango is done.
4. Add the ground masala and cook till the raw smell disappears. Remove from the heat and set aside.
5. In the meantime, cook the rice on a platter by spreading it.
6. Add the salt, curry leaves, and stir in the cooked masala little by little, till the masala blends completely with the rice.
7. Serve hot.

Ingredients
- 1/2 kg raw rice
- 1 cup water
- Salt to taste

METHOD

1. Soak rice in water for 4 hrs then dry it, then grind it to make fine powder. Heat the powder for 10 mins until the powder becomes light brown. Sieve the powder.

2. Mix hot water and salt to make a smooth ball. Put this in a idiyyapam maker and make it in a thread like form.

3. Put this in a iddli maker after applying oil and cook it for 2 mins in a cooker. Idiyyappam can be served with stew curry.

Idiyappam

Lemon Rice

Lemon Rice
(Elumichampaza Sadam)

87

Ingredients
- 1 cup long-grained rice
- Juice of 2 lemons
- ¼ teaspoon turmeric powder
- 2 green chillies, chopped fine
- 1-inch piece ginger, chopped fine
- Salt to taste
- Chopped coriander leaves for garnishing

For Tempering
- 1 teaspoon mustard seeds
- 1 teaspoon cumin seeds
- 1 teaspoon black gram dhal
- 1 teaspoon bengal gram dhal
- 1 red chilli, halved
- ½ teaspoon asafoetida powder
- A few curry leaves

METHOD

1. Cook the rice and set aside
2. Heat the pan. Add all the ingredients for tempering. When the mustard seeds splutter, add the green chillies, ginger and roast for a couple of minutes.
3. Add the rice, turmeric powder and salt. Mix well.
4. Turn off the heat and add the lemon juice.
5. Garnish with chopped coriander leaves and serve hot.

88 Black Gram Dal Rice
(Ulundu Ogaray)

Ingredients
- 1 cup raw rice
- Salt to taste

Dry Masala
- 2 tablespoons black gram dhal
- 1 ½ teaspoons peppercorns
- 2 tablespoons sesame seeds

For tempering
- 1 teaspoon mustard seeds
- 1 teaspoon black gram dhal
- 1 teaspoon bengal gram dhal
- 1 red chilli, halved
- ½ teaspoon asafoetida powder
- 2 green chillies, chopped fine
- A few curry leaves

METHOD

1. Cook the rice and set aside.

2. Roast dry the ingredients for the dry masala. Powder fine and set aside.

3. Heat the pan, add the mustard seeds, bengal gram dhal, black gram dal, slit red chilli, asafoetida powder and curry leaves. When the mustard seeds splutter, add the chopped green chillies.

4. Add the cooked rice. Sprinkle the dry masala powder and salt.

Mustard Seeds Rice
(Kadugu Ogaray)

89

Ingredients
- 1 cup long-grained rice
- Salt to taste

Paste
- 1 tablespoon mustard seeds
- 4 red chillies
- ½ teaspoon turmeric powder
- ½ teaspoon asafoetida powder
- Marble-sized tamarind

For tempering
- 1 teaspoon mustard seeds
- 1 ½ teaspoon black gram dhal
- 1 ½ teaspoons bengal gram dhal
- 1 red chilli, halved
- A few curry leaves

METHOD

1. Pressure cook the rice and set aside
2. Grind fine all the ingredients for the paste, using a little water.
3. Heat the pan adds all the ingredients for tempering. When the mustard seeds splutter, roast for a couple of minutes.
4. Add the paste and roast till the raw smell disappears.
5. Add the rice, salt and stir to mix.
6. Serve hot.

90 | Spicy Sambar Rice
(Bissi Bele Hulli Anna)

Ingredients
- 1 cup rice
- 1 cup red gram dhal
- ½ cup small sambar onions, peeled
- 1 capsicum, diced fine
- 1 small brinjal, diced fine
- 2 tablespoons fresh peas (optional)
- 1 potato, diced fine
- ½ teaspoon turmeric powder
- Lime-sized tamarind
- 1 small bunch coriander leaves
- Chopped for garnishing
- Salt to taste

Paste
- 12-14 red chillies
- 3 tablespoons coriander seeds
- 3 teaspoons bengal gram dhal
- 1 inch piece cinnamon
- 1 ½ teaspoons poppy seeds
- 4 cloves
- ½ teaspoon fenugreek seeds
- 1 teaspoon asafoetida powder

Dry Masala
- 3 tablespoons gram dhal
- 1 ½ teaspoons poppy seeds
- 3 teaspoons rice

For Tempering
- 1 teaspoon mustard seeds
- 1 teaspoon cumin seeds
- 1 tablespoon split black gram dhal
- 1 tablespoon bengal gram dhal
- 1 red chilli, halved
- A few curry leaves

METHOD

1. Pressure cook the rice and dal in 4 cups of water and set aside in the pressure cooker itself so that the heat is not lost.
2. Roast all the ingredients for the paste in pan and grind to a fine paste using very little water.
3. Roast dry all the ingredients for the dry masala and powder fine.
4. Soak the tamarind in 2 cups water, extract the juice and set aside.
5. Heat a heavy bottomed vessel and add all the ingredients for tempering.
6. When the mustard seeds splutter, add the onions and roast for a couple for minutes. Add the rest of the vegetables and cook till the vegetables are partly cooked.
7. Add the tamarind juice, salt, turmeric powder and cook till the vegetables are tender.
8. Add the paste to the vegetables and cook for a couple of minutes. Set aside the sambar.
9. In a heavy frying pan or pressure cooker, add the rice and dhal. Take care that no lumps are formed.
10. Simmer on a low heat and cook till the mixture blends.
11. Add the dry masala and remove from the heat.
12. Garnish with chopped coriander leaves and serve hot.

(Famous in Tamil Nadu)

<table>
<tr><td>

91

</td><td>

Seasame Seed Powder
(Ellu Podi)

</td></tr>
</table>

Ingredients

1 cup white sesame seeds

10-12 red chillies

1 teaspoon asafoetida powder

Salt to taste

METHOD

1. Roast all the ingredients in the pan and powder coarse in a grinder. Add salt.

2. Serve with plain hot rice.

92 Green Peas Rice
(Pattani Sadam)

Ingredients
- 1 cup long-grained rice
- 1 cup shelled green peas
- 1 small potato, peeled and chopped fine
- 2 small brinjals, chopped fine
- 1 capsicum, chopped fine
- 1 teaspoon turmeric powder
- Marble-sized tamarind
- Salt to taste

Masala
- 3 tablespoons coriander seeds
- 2 tablespoons black gram dhal
- 3 tablespoons bengal gram dhal
- ½ teaspoon asafoetida powder
- 5 red chillies

For Tempering
- 2 teaspoons mustard seeds
- 1 teaspoon black gram dhal
- 1 teaspoon bengal gram dhal
- 1 red chilli, halved
- A few curry leaves

METHOD

1. Pressure cook the rice and set aside to cool.

2. **To make the masala :** Heat the pan and roast all the ingredients for the masala. Powder fine, adding the tamarind.

3. Heat the pan and add all the ingredients for tempering. When the mustard seeds splutter, add the peas potatoes, brinjals and capsicum. Cook on a low heat till the vegetables are done, adding water if necessary.

4. Add the powdered masala, turmeric powder and salt. Roast for a minute or two.

5. Add the rice and mix well till everything blends.

6. Serve hot.

Green Peas Rice

Rice Pongal

93 | Rice Pongal
(Ven Pongal)

Ingredients
- 1 cup raw rice
- ½ cup green gram dhal
- 1 teaspoon cumin seeds
- 1 teaspoon peppercorns
- 1 teaspoon asafoetida powder
- ½ teaspoon turmeric powder
- 4 ½ cups of water
- 1 inch piece ginger, grated
- A few curry leaves
- Salt to taste

METHOD
1. Powder coarsely the cumin seeds and peppercorns. Set aside.
2. Roast the rice as well as green gram dhal separately. Mix together, wash well, and add the turmeric powder and 4 ½ cups water. Pressure cook and set aside.
3. Heat the pan. Add the cumin seeds, peppercorns, asafoetida powder, grated ginger and curry leaves.
4. Add the cooked rice and dal and mix well. Add salt.
5. Serve hot with spicy tamarind kuzhambu.

Dal Powder
(Parupu Podi)

Ingredients
- 1 cup red gram dhal
- 1 tablespoon bengal gram dhal
- 1 tablespoon black gram dhal
- ¾ tablespoon peppercorns
- 1 teaspoon cumin seeds
- 5 red chillies
- ½ teaspoon asafoetida powder
- Salt to taste

METHOD

1. Roast dry the red gram dhal, bengal gram dhal and black gram dhal for four to five minutes on a low heat.

2. Roast the peppercorns, cumin seeds, red chillies and asafoetida powder.

3. Powder everything in a dry grinder, adding salt as required.

4. Serve with hot rice.

Dhal Powder

Ordinary Vadai

Ordinary Vadai
(Medu Vadai)

95

Ingredients
- 1 cup black gram dhal
- 4 green chillies
- 1 teaspoon asafoetida powder
- 1 bunch coriander leaves, chopped fine
- Salt to taste

METHOD

1. Soak the black gram dhal in 2 cups of water for two hours. Drain off excess water, completely. Add the green chillies, salt and asafoetida powder, grind to a smooth batter, using very little water.

2. Add the chopped coriander leaves to the batter. Mix well.

3. **To make the vadais :** Heat idli mould. Take a ladleful of batter and place it on the palm of the left hand. Flatten the batter with the wet right hand. Make a hole in the center. Slip gently into the idli mould. Steam it

4. Roast till golden brown and bake in an over till crisp.

5. Serve hot with chutney.

96 Curry Leaves Powder
(Karivepilai Podi)

Ingredients
- 1 big bunch curry leaves (30-35)
- 1 cup coriander seeds
- 1 tablespoon peppercorns
- 1 tablespoon cumin seeds
- ½ tablespoon fenugreek seeds
- ½ tablespoon mustard seeds
- 1 tablespoon black gram dhal
- 1 tablespoon bengal gram dhal
- 1 teaspoon asafoetida powder
- 2 tablespoons jaggery, powdered
- Marble-sized tamarind
- Salt to taste

METHOD
1. Roast the curry leaves for a couple of minutes. Set aside.
2. Roast the coriander seeds, peppercorns, cumin seeds, fenugreek seeds, mustard seeds, black gram dhal, bengal gram dhal and asafoetida powder till the dhals turn golden.
3. Powder fine everything in a grinder adding the jaggery, tamarind and salt.
4. Serve with hot rice.

97

Kancheepuram Idli

Ingredients
- 1 ½ cups parboiled rice
- 1 cup black gram dhal
- ½ teaspoon asafoetida powder
- 1 teaspoon crushed peppercorns
- 1 ½ teaspoons crushed dry ginger
- 1 teaspoon cumin seeds
- A few curry leaves
- Salt to taste

METHOD

1. Soak the parboiled rice and black gram dhal in water for a couple of hours.

2. Grind the rice and black gram dhal to a coarse batter. Add the asafoetida powder, crushed peppercorns, ginger, cumin seeds and salt and allow to ferment for twenty-four hours. The batter should become sour.

3. Just before making the idlis, heat the pan and add the cury leaves. Remove from the heat, mix well with the idli batter.

4. Smear water in a pan. Pour the batter and pressure cook without the weight for twenty minutes till done.

5. Cut into triangles. Serve hot with chutney.

98

Semolina Dosai
(Rava Dosai)

Ingredients

- 1 cup refined flour
- 1 cup semolina
- 1 cup rice flour
- 2 teaspoons cumin seeds
- 3-4 green chillies, chopped fine
- 1 cup sour curd, salt to taste
- A small bunch coriander leaves, chopped fine
- A few curry leaves
- Water for mixing

METHOD

1. Mix all the three flours. Add the salt, cumin seeds, green chillies, sour curd, coriander and curry leaves, and enough water to form a stiff dough.
2. Set aside for at least two hours.
3. Add some more water to make a dosai batter of thin pouring consistency. (It should be thinner than the ordinary dosai batter.)
4. To prepare the tawa : Heat the tawa. Sprinkle a few drops of water. If it sizzles, the tawa is ready for use.
5. Heat the tawa. Put some water. When the water evaporates lower the heat.
6. To make the dosais : Pour a ladleful of batter on the outer edges of the tawa. Continue to pour inwards, using a circular motion to make a dosai which measures 5-6 inches. Smoothen gently with the back of the ladle to remove lumps if any.
7. Cook both sides till golden. The cooked dosai will have small holes over its surface.
8. Serve hot with chutney.

99 | Wheat Flour Dosai
(Godumai Dosai)

Ingredients

- 2 cups wheat flour
- 1 cup rice flour
- ½ cup sour buttermilk
- 2 green chillies, chopped fine
- 1 small bunch coriander leaves, chopped fine
- Salt to taste
- Sufficient water to make a batter of pouring
- Consistency

For Tempering

- ½ teaspoon mustard seeds
- ½ teaspoon cumin seeds
- ¼ teaspoon asafoetida powder
- A few curry leaves

METHOD

1. Mix the wheat flour and rice flour with the sour buttermilk and add sufficient water to make a batter of pouring consistency. Add the chopped chillies and coriander leaves.

2. Heat the pan and add all the ingredients for tempering. When the mustard seeds splutter, add the seasoning to the dosai batter. Add salt and mix well.

4. **To prepare the tawa :** Heat the tawa. Sprinkle a few drops of water. If it sizzles, the tawa is ready for use.

4. Heat the tawa. Put some water. When the water evaporates lower the heat.

5. To make the dosais : Pour a ladleful of batter on the outer edges of the tawa. Continue to pour inwards, using a circular motion to make a dosai which measures 5-6 inches. Smoothen gently with the back of the ladle to remove lumps if any.

6. Serve hot

100

Ragi Dosai

Ingredients

- 2 cups ragi flour
- ½ cup rice flour
- ½ cup sour curd
- 3-4 green chillies, chopped fine
- 1 bunch coriander leaves, chopped fine
- 1 onion, chopped fine (optional)
- Salt to taste
- 1 teaspoon mustard seeds
- 1 teaspoon cumin seeds
- ½ teaspoon asafoetida powder
- A few curry leaves

METHOD

1. Mix the ragi flour, rice flour, salt, chopped coriander leaves, green chillies and onion. Add sufficient water to form a batter of thin pouring consistency. Set aside for two hours.
2. Heat the pan and add all the ingredients for tempering. When the mustard seeds splutter, add to the batter.
3. **To prepare the tawa :** Heat the tawa. Sprinkle a few drops of water. If it sizzles, the tawa is ready for use.
4. Heat the tawa. Put some water. When the water evaporates, lower the heat.
5. To make the dosais : Pour a ladleful of batter on the outer edges of the tawa. Continue to pour inwards, using a circular motion to make a dosai which measures 5-6 inches. Smoothen gently with the back of the ladle to remove lumps if any.
6. Serve hot with chutney.

101   Jaggery Dosai
(Vella Dosai)

Ingredients

- 2 cups wheat flour
- 1 cup rice flour
- 1 cup jaggery, powdered
- 1 cup water

METHOD

1. In a heavy-bottomed vessel heat the jaggery and water. Simmer on a low heat till well blended. Remove from the heat, strain, and cool.

2. Add the jaggery syrup to the wheat flour and the rice flour to make a batter of thin pouring consistency. Add water if necessary.

3. **To prepare the tawa :** Heat the tawa. Sprinkle a few drops of water. If it sizzles, the tawa is ready for use.

4. Heat the tawa. Put some water. When the water evaporates, lower the heat.

4. **To make the dosais :** Pour a ladleful of batter on the outer edges of the tawa. Continue to pour inwards, using a circular motion to make a dosai which measures 5-6 inches. Smoothen gently with the back of the ladle to remove lumps if any.

6. Serve hot. For those who like the sweet and sour taste, serve with Instant Mango Pickle.

102 Potato Dosai
(Urulaikizhangu Dosai)

Ingredients

- 1 cup rice flour
- 2 large potatoes
- ½ cup sour curd
- 2 green chillies, chopped fine
- 1 small bunch coriander leaves
- Salt to taste

METHOD

1. Boil the potatoes in their jackets; peel and mash well.

2. In a mixing bowl, blend the mashed potatoes, flour, curd, green chillies, coriander leaves and salt. Add sufficient water to form a batter of pouring consistency.

3. **To prepare the tawa :** Heat the tawa. Sprinkle a few drops of water. If it sizzles, the tawa is ready for use.

4. Heat the tawa. Put some water. When the water evaporates, lower the heat.

5. **To make the dosai :** Pour a ladleful of batter on the outer edges of the tawa. Continue to pour inwards, using a circular motion to make a dosai which measures 5-6 inches. Smoothen gently with the back of the ladle to remove lumps if any.

6. Serve hot with chutney.

103

Dhal Dosai
(Adai)

Ingredients
- ½ cup black gram dhal
- ½ cup red gram dal
- ½ cup bengal gram dhal
- 1 cup raw rice.
- 4-6 red chillies
- 1 large onion, chopped fine
- ½ teaspoon asafoetida powder
- 1 bunch chopped coriander leaves
- Salt to taste

METHOD

1. Soak the black gram dhal, red gram dhal, bengal gram dhal, raw rice and red chillies in 2 cups of water for two hours.
2. Grind coarsely.
3. Add the salt, chopped onion, coriander leaves and asafoetida powder.
4. **To prepare the tawa :** Heat the tawa. Sprinkle a few drops of water. If it sizzles, the tawa is ready for use.
5. Heat the tawa. Put some water. When the water evaporates, lower the heat.
6. **To make the dal dosais :** Pour a ladleful of batter and spread like a dosai, as thin as possible. Make a hole in the center. Cook till golden brown in color
7. Turn the other side and roast till golden and crisp.
8. Serve hot with chutney.

104

Green Gram Dosai
(Pesarattu)

Ingredients

- 2 cups green gram dhal
- ½ cup ordinary raw rice
- 5 green chillies
- 1 big onion, chopped fine
- 1 potato, boiled and mashed (optional)
- 1 bunch coriander leaves, chopped fine
- 1/ teaspoon asafoetida powder
- Salt to taste

METHOD

1. Soak the green gram dhal and rice in water for forty-five minutes and grind coarsely in a liquidizer (mixie) along with the green chillies.

2. To the ground batter add the salt, asafoetida powder, chopped onions, mashed potato and coriander leaves and mix well to make a batter of thick dropping consistency.

3. **To prepare the tawa :** Heat the tawa. Sprinkle a few drops of water. If it sizzles, the tawa is ready for use.

4. Heat the tawa. Put some water. When the water evaporates lower the heat.

5. **To make the dosais :** Pour a ladleful of batter on the outer edges of the tawa. Continue to pour inwards, using a circular motion to make a dosai which measures 5-6 inches. Smoothen gently with the back of the ladle to remove lumps if any.

6. Serve hot with chutney.

105

Spicy Dosai
(Kara Dosai)

Ingredients

- 1 cup ordinary raw rice
- ½ cup red gram dhal
- 6 red chillies
- ½ teaspoon asafoetida powder
- Salt to taste

METHOD

1. Soak the rice and dhal in 3 cups of water for two hours.

2. Grind the soaked rice and dhal to a fine batter, add the red chillies, asafoetida powder and salt. Add enough water if necessary.

3. **To prepare the tawa :** Heat the tawa. Sprinkle a few drops of water. If it sizzles, the tawa is ready for use.

4. Heat the tawa. Put some water. When the water evaporates, lower the heat.

5. To make the dosais : Pour a ladleful of batter on the outer edges of the tawa. Continue to pour inwards, using a circular motion to make a dosai which measures 5-6 inches. Smoothen gently with the back of the ladle to remove lumps if any.

6. Serve hot with chutney.

(Famous in Kerala)

Semolina Adai
(Rava Adai)

106

Ingredients

- 1³/₄ cup semolina, roasted
- 4 green chilies, chopped fine
- ½ inch piece ginger grated fine
- ½ teaspoon sugar
- 1 teaspoon cumin seeds
- 1 tablespoon well mixed curd
- salt to taste

METHOD

1. In a mixing bowl, add all the ingredients except the semolina. Add the sufficient water and mix well. Finally add all the semolina and mix well to make a batter of thick dropping consistency. Add more water if necessary.

2. **To prepare the tawa :** Heat the tawa. Sprinkle a few drops of water. If it sizzles, the tawa is ready for use.

3. Heat the tawa. Put some water. When the water evaporates, lower the heat.

4. **To make the dal dosais :** Pour a ladleful of batter and spread like a dosai, as thin as possible. Make a hole in the center. Cook till golden brown in color.

5. Serve hot with chutney

107 Rice Idli
(Idli)

Ingredients
- 2 cups parboiled rice
- 1 cup black gram dhal
- salt to taste

METHOD

1. Soak the parboiled rice and black gram dhal separately for four to five hours.

2. Grind the soaked dhal to a very fine batter.

3. Grind the rice into a batter, a little more coarse than the dhal.

4. Mix the dhal and rice batter, add the salt and set aside to ferment for at least eight hours.

5. Steam in idli moulds in a pressure cooker for fifteen minutes (without weight). Do not stir the batter before filling the moulds. It is the trapped air that makes fluffy, soft idlis.

6. Serve hot with chutney and small onion sambar.

Rice Idli

Semolina Idli

108 Semolina Idli
(Rava Idli)

Ingredients
- 1 cup fine semolina
- 1 inch piece ginger, skinned and grated
- 2 green chillies, chopped fine
- 1 small bunch coriander leaves, chopped fine
- ½ cup sour curd
- Salt to taste
- Water as required

For Tempering
- 1 teaspoon mustard seeds
- 1 teaspoon cumin seeds
- A few curry leaves.

METHOD

1. Heat the pan and roast the semolina till golden. Set aside.
2. Mix the semolina, ginger, chillies, coriander leaves, sour curd and salt, using very little water. The batter should be of a thick pouring consistency.
3. Heat the pan and add all the ingredients for tempering. When the mustard seeds splutter, add to the batter. Mix well.
4. Pressure cook in an idli mould like Rice Idli.
5. Serve hot with chutney.

(Famous in Tamil Nadu & Karnataka)

109   Vegetable Rava Uppuma

Ingredients

- 1 cup semolina
- 2 onions, chopped fine
- Mixed chopped vegetables (1 potato, 1 capsicum, 1 small carrot and 3 beans)
- ¼ cup shelled peas (optional)
- ½ inch piece ginger scraped and chopped fine
- 2-3 green chillies, chopped fine
- ½ teaspoon turmeric powder
- 1 small bunch coriander leaves, chopped fine
- 3 cups water
- Juice of 1 lemon
- Salt to taste

For Tempering

- 1 teaspoon mustard seeds
- 1 teaspoon cumin seeds
- 1 teaspoon black gram dhal
- 1 teaspoon bengal gram dhal
- ½ teaspoon asafoetida powder
- 1 red chilli, halved
- A few curry leaves

METHOD

1. Dry roast the semolina lightly and set aside.

2. Heat a pan and add all the ingredients for tempering. When the mustard seeds splutter, add the chopped onions, ginger, green chillies and sauté for a minute or two.

3. Add the chopped vegetables, salt and turmeric powder and roast for another minute.

4. Add the 3 cups of water, simmer covered on a low heat till the vegetables are tender.

5. Add the semolina gradually. Take care to prevent lumps. Cook until the water is completely absorbed. Turn off the heat.

6. Add the lemon juice. Garnish with coriander leaves.

7. Serve hot.

Cabbage Vada
(Cabbage Vadai)

110

Ingredients

- ½ cup cabbage, chopped fine
- 2 tablespoons shelled peas (optional)
- 1 cup black gram dhal
- 1 big onion, chopped fine
- 4 green chillies
- 1 teaspoon asafoetida powder
- 1 bunch coriander leaves, chopped fine
- Salt to taste.

METHOD

1. Soak the black gram dhal in 2 cups of water for two hours. Drain well.

2. Grind the black gram dhal to a smooth batter, adding the green chillies, salt and asafoetida powder.

3. Add the chopped onions, cabbage, coriander leaves and peas to the batter. Mix well.

4. **To make the vadais :** Heat idli mould. Take a ladleful of batter and place it on the palm of the left hand. Flatten the batter with the wet right hand. Make a hole in the center. Slip gently into the idli mould. Steam it

5. Serve hot with chutney.

111 Masala Vadai

Ingredients

- ½ cup red gram dhal
- ½ cup black gram dhal
- ½ cup bengal gram dhal
- 6 red chillies
- 4 green chillies, chopped fine
- ½ teaspoon asafoetida powder.
- ½ cup onions, chopped fine
- 1 inch piece ginger, chopped fine
- 1 bunch coriander leaves, chopped fine
- A few curry leaves
- Salt to taste

METHOD

1. Soak the red gram dhal, black gram dhal and bengal gram dhal in water for an hour. Drain off excess water, completely.
2. Grind the soaked dhals along with the red chillies to a coarse batter.
3. Add the salt, chopped onions, curry leaves, coriander leaves, green chillies, asafoetida powder and ginger to the batter.
4. **To make the vadais :** Heat idli mould. Take a ladleful of batter and place it on the palm of the left hand. Flatten the batter with the wet right hand. Make a hole in the center. Slip gently into the idli mould. Steam it
5. It is not necessary to make a hole in the center of the vadai.
6. Serve hot with chutney.

112   Mysore Vadai

Ingredients

- ½ cup rice flour
- ½ cup fine semolina
- ½ cup refined flour
- 4-5 green chillies, chopped fine
- 2 medium sized onions, chopped fine
- 1 small bunch coriander leaves, chopped fine
- ½ teaspoon asafoetida powder
- Salt to taste
- Water as required

METHOD

1. Mix all the ingredients together. Add sufficient water to make a stiff batter.

2. **To make the vadais :** Heat idli mould. Take a ladleful of batter and place it on the palm of the left hand. Flatten the batter with the wet right hand. Make a hole in the center. Slip gently into the idli mould. Steam it

3. Serve hot with mint chutney.

Potato Bonda

(Urulaikizhangu Vadai)

113

Ingredients

- 4 big potatoes
- 2 big onions, diced fine
- 1-inch piece ginger, chopped fine
- 4 green chillies, chopped fine
- 1 bunch coriander leaves, chopped fine
- ½ teaspoon turmeric powder
- Salt to taste

Batter

- 2 cups bengal gram flour
- 2 teaspoons red chilli powder
- ½ teaspoon asafoetida powder
- Salt to taste

For Tempering

- 1 teaspoon mustard seeds
- 1 teaspoon black gram dhal
- 1 red chilli, halved
- A few curry leaves

METHOD

1. Boil the potatoes in their jackets. Peel and mash.
2. Add the bengal gram flour, rice flour, shredded ginger, green chillies, coriander leaves, asafoetida powder and curry leaves.
3. Heat the pan and add the mustard seeds. When they splutter, add to the potato mixture. Mix well.
4. **To make the vadais :** Heat idli mould. Take a ladleful of batter and place it on the palm of the left hand. Flatten the batter with the wet right hand. Make a hole in the center. Slip gently into the idli mould. Steam it
5. Serve hot with chutney.

114

Sago Vadai
(Javarisi Vadai)

Ingredients

- ½ cup sago
- ½ cup sour buttermilk
- ½ cup bengal gram flour or rice flour
- 1 teaspoon red chilli powder
- ½ teaspoon asafoetida powder
- 2 green chillies, chopped fine
- A small bunch coriander leaves, chopped fine
- Salt to taste

METHOD

1. Soak the sago in the buttermilk for half an hour.

2. Add the bengal gram flour or rice flour, salt, red chilli powder green chillies and asafoetida powder to make a stiff batter. Add water if necessary.

3. **To make the vadais :** Heat idli mould. Take a ladleful of batter and place it on the palm of the left hand. Flatten the batter with the wet right hand. Make a hole in the center. Slip gently into the idli mould. Steam it

4. Serve hot with chutney.

Potato Bonda
(Urulaikizhangu Bonda)

115

Ingredients

- 4 big potatoes
- 2 big onions, diced fine
- 1 inch piece ginger, chopped fine
- 4 green chillies, chopped fine
- 1 bunch coriander leaves, chopped fine
- ½ teaspoon turmeric powder
- Salt to taste

Batter

2 cups bengal gram flour

2 teaspoons red chilli powder

½ teaspoon asafoetida powder

Salt to taste

For Tempering

1 teaspoon mustard seeds

1 teaspoon black gram dhal

1 red chilli, halved

A few curry leaves

METHOD

1. Boil the potatoes in their jackets. Peel, mash and set aside.

2. Heat the pan and add all the ingredients for tempering. When the mustard seeds splutter, add the chopped green chillies, ginger, and onions and roast for a couple of minutes.

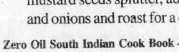

3. Add the mashed potatoes, salt, turmeric powder and chopped coriander leaves. Cook for a couple of minutes till well blended. Remove from the heat and cool.

4. Shape the potato mixture into lemon-sized rounds. Set aside.

5. **To make the batter :** Mix all the ingredients for the batter. Add sufficient water to make a smooth batter of dropping consistency.

6. Heat the pan. Dip each round into the batter and roast & bake till golden brown.

7. Serve hot with chutney.

116

Mysore Bonda

Ingredients
- 1 cup black gram dhal
- 1 teaspoon whole peppercorns
- ½ teaspoon asafoetida powder
- salt to taste
- a few curry leaves

METHOD

1. Soak the black gram dhal in 2 cups of water for 2 hours. Drain well.

2. Grind the black gram dhal to a smooth batter. Add the salt, peppercorns, asafoetida powder, curry leaves.

3. Heat the idli stand. Shape the batter into small balls, the size of lemons, and drop gently into the idli stand. Steam it and bake till golden brown.

4. Serve hot with chutney

117 Vegetable Bonda

Ingredients

- 1 cup bengal gram dhal
- 4 red chillies
- 1 teaspoon asafoetida powder
- ½ cup cauliflower flowerets
- ¼ cup green peas
- 1 onion chopped fine
- a few curry leaves
- salt to taste

METHOD

1. Soak the bengal gram dhal in 2 cups of water for an hour. Drain well.

2. Grind the soaked dhal to a fine batter, adding the red chillies, asafoetida powder, and salt.

3. Mix the chopped vegetables and curry leaves to the batter.

4. Heat the idli stand. Shape the batter into small balls, the size of lemons, and drop gently into the idli stand. Steam it and bake till golden brown and crisp.

5. Serve hot with chutney.

Colocasia Bondai
(Chepangkizhangu Bonda)

118

Ingredients
- ½ kg colocasia
- 6 green chillies
- ½ inch piece ginger, scraped
- 1 tablespoon sour curd
- ½ teaspoon asafoetida powder
- A small bunch coriander leaves, chopped fine
- Salt to taste

Batter
- 1 cup refined flour
- ½ cup bengal gram flour
- ½ cup rice flour
- A pinch of soda-bi-carbonate
- Salt to taste

METHOD

1. Grind together the green chillies, ginger and coriander leaves into a fine paste.
2. Pressure cook the colocasia; peel and chop fine
3. Add the paste, salt asafoetida powder and curds. Mix well. Set aside.
4. Make a batter of thick pouring consistency with the bengal gram flour, refined flour, rice flour, salt, a pinch of soda-bi-carbonate and sufficient water.
5. Heat idli mould. Shape the colocasia mixture into small balls, dip into the batter in an idle mould , steam it and bake till golden.

(Famous in Tamil Nadu)

119   Vegetable Bajji

Ingredients
Batter
- 1 cup bengal gram flour
- 1 teaspoon red chilli powder
- ½ teaspoon cumin seeds
- ½ teaspoon coriander seeds powder
- ½ teaspoon asafoetida powder
- 1 ½ tablespoons rice flour
- Salt to taste

Any of the following vegetables can be used
- 1 green raw plantain, peeled and cut into thin slices
- 1 potato, peeled and sliced
- 1 onion, peeled and sliced
- 1 chow chow, peeled and sliced
- 1 ridge gourd, peeled and sliced
- Cauliflower cut into flowerets

METHOD

1. Mix all the ingredients for the batter. Add sufficient water and beat until smooth to make a thick batter of pouring consistency.
2. Wash the vegetable slices and pat dry.
3. Heat the idli mould: Dip the vegetable slices in the batter and steam in the idli mould.
4. Bake till brown.
5. Serve hot with tomato ketchup or chutney.

            Zero Oil South Indian Cook Book

120

Onion Pakoda
(Vengaya Pakoda)

Ingredients

- 1 cup bengal gram flour
- ½ rice flour
- 3 onions, chopped fine
- 1 potato, chopped fine (optional)
- 1 inch piece ginger, scraped and chopped fine
- 4 green chillies, chopped fine
- 1 tablespoon red chilli powder
- 1 bunch coriander leaves, chopped fine
- A pinch of soda-bi-carbonate
- Salt to taste

METHOD

1. In a mixing bowl rub the soda till frothy. Add all the ingredients and make a stiff batter, using sufficient water.

2. Heat the idli mould. Drop spoonfuls of the batter into the idli mould steam it and bake till golden in colour.

3. Serve hot with tomato ketchup or chutney.

121   Oothappam

Ingredients
- 2 cups leftover sour dosai batter
- 1 onion, chopped fine
- 1 tomato, chopped fine
- 1-2 green chillies, chopped fine
- A small bunch coriander leaves, chopped fine

METHOD

1. Mix the chopped onions, tomatoes, green chillies and coriander leaves. Set aside.
2. To prepare the tawa : Heat the tawa. Sprinkle a few drops of water. If it sizzles, the tawa is ready for use.
3. Heat the tawa. Put some water. When the water evaporates lower the heat.
4. To make the Oothappam : Pour a ladleful of batter to make a thick dosai (1/4 inch). Do not spread out the batter thin.
5. Sprinkle evenly a tablespoon of the vegetable mixture over the dosai. Roast till golden.
6. Turn the dosai carefully and roast till done.
7. Serve hot with chutney.

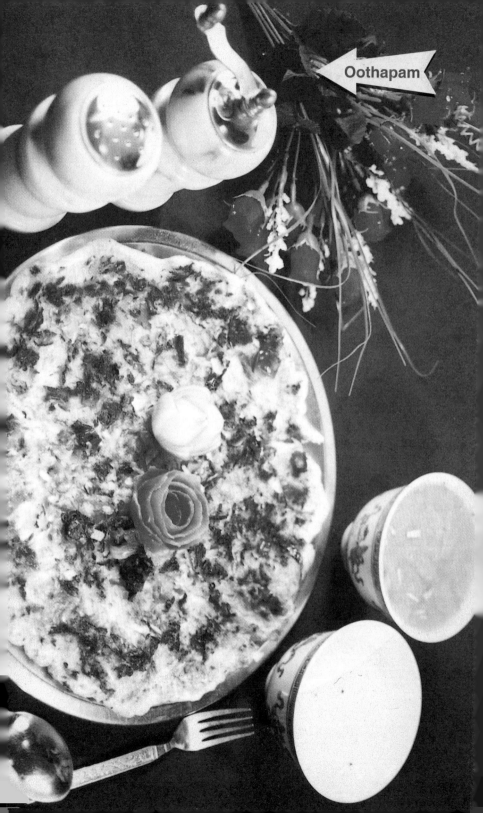

Oothapam

Ordinary Dosai

Ordinary Dosai
(Dosai)

122

Ingredients

- 3 cups parboiled rice
- 1 cup black gram dhal
- 2 teaspoons fenugreek seeds
- Salt to taste

METHOD

1. Soak the parboiled rice in water for at least six hours. Make a smooth batter in a liquidizer (mixie).
2. Soak together the black gram dhal and fenugreek seeds, also for six hours. Make a smooth batter.
3. Mix the batters together, adding salt and set aside for at least twelve hours till the mixture ferments. Use a large pot since the batter is likely to increase in volume when fermented. The batter should become a mass of tiny bubbles. Do not stir too much.
4. To prepare the tawa (griddle) : Heat the tawa. Sprinkle a few drops of water. If it sizzles, the tawa is ready for use.
5. Heat the tawa. Put some water. When the water evaporates lower the heat.
6. To make the dosais : Pour a ladleful of batter over the tawa and spread quickly using a continous spiral motion, spreading it outwards till the dosai measures about 6 inches.
7. Increase the heat and cook for a couple of minutes till golden brown in colour.
8. Turn the dosai, carefully lifting the edges. Roast for another couple of minutes till done.
9. Serve hot.

123 | Beaten Rice Uppuma
(Aval Uppuma)

Ingredients

- ¼ kg beaten rice
- 2 potatoes, peeled and chopped fine
- 2 onions, diced fine
- 4 green chillies, chopped fine
- ½ teaspoon turmeric powder
- Salt to taste
- A small bunch coriander leves for garnishing
- Juice of 1 lemon (optional)

For Tempering

- 1 teaspoon mustard seeds
- 1 teaspoon cumin seeds
- ¼ teaspoon asafoetida powder
- 1 red chilli, halved
- A few curry leaves

METHOD

1. Wash the beaten rice thoroughly. Drain and set aside.
2. Heat the karahi and add all the ingredients for tempering. When the mustard seeds splutter, add the chopped onion, green chillies and sauté for a minute or two.
3. Add the chopped potatoes, turmeric powder and salt. Sprinkle some water and cook till the vegetable is tender.
4. Add the beaten rice, stir well and cook till all the water is absorbed and the mixture is completely dry.
5. Turn off the heat. Add the lemon juice and garnish with chopped coriander leaves.
6. Serve hot.

124

Sundal

Ingredients

- 1 cup chickpeas
- ½ raw mango, peeled and chopped fine
- 1 green chilli, chopped fine
- Juice of 1 lemon
- Salt to taste

For Tempering

- 1 teaspoon mustard seeds
- 1 teaspoon black gram dhal
- 1 red chilli, halved
- ½ teaspoon asafoetida powder

METHOD

1. Soak the chickpeas for seven to eight hours. Pressure cook, drain and set aside.

2. Heat the pan and add all the ingredients for tempering. When the mustard seeds splutter, add the boiled chickpeas.

3. Add the chopped mango, green chilli and salt. Mix well. Turn off the heat. Add the lemon juice.

4. Serve hot or cold.

125 Colocasia Chips
(Chepangkizhangu Varuval)

Ingredients
- 1 Kg colocasia
- 10 red chillies
- ½ teaspoon turmeric powder
- 1 teaspoon asafoetida powder
- marble sized tamarind
- salt to taste

METHOD

1. Pressure-cook the colocasia with their jackets. Peel and chop into ½ inch pieces.

2. Grind to a fine paste the turmeric powder, red chillies, asafoetida powder, salt and tamarind, adding a very little water.

3. Smear the paste evenly over the cooked colocasia pieces.

4. Heat the pan and roast. Bake at 200°C for 3 minutes.

5. Serve hot.

Yam Chips

(Chenaikizhangu Varuval)

126

Ingredients

- 1 kg yam
- 2 teaspoons chilli powder
- 2 teaspoons turmeric powder
- 1 teaspoon asafoetida powder
- Salt to taste
- 4 cups water

METHOD

1. Add the turmeric powder to the 4 cups of water and set aside.

2. Peel the yam and slice thinly. Immerse in the turmeric solution for thirty minutes.

3. Drain, pat dry and spread on a thin cloth.

4. Heat the pan and roast. Bake at 200° C for 3 minutes.

5. Mix the salt, chilli powder and asafoetida powder. Sprinkle on the chips.

Store in an airtight container.

127

Masala Dosai

Ingredients

For Dosai

- 3 cups parboiled rice
- 1 cup black gram dhal
- Fenugreek seeds

For Masala

- ½ Kg potatoes
- ½ cup boiled peas
- 2 medium sized onions, chopped fine
- 2-3 inch piece ginger, scrapped and chopped fine
- ½ teaspoon turmeric powder
- 2 tomatoes chopped fine
- salt to taste
- a small bunch coriander leaves chopped fine

METHOD

1. Soak the parboiled rice in water for at least six hours. Make a smooth batter in a liquidizer (mixie).

2. Soak together the black gram dhal and fenugreek seeds, also for six hours. Make a smooth batter.

3. Mix the batters together, adding salt and set aside for at least twelve hours till the mixture ferments. Use a large pot, since the batter is likely to increase in volume when fermented. The batter should become a mass of tiny bubbles. Do not stir too much.

4. **To prepare the tawa :** Heat the tawa. Sprinkle a few drops of water. If it sizzles, the tawa is ready for use.

5. Heat the tawa. Put some water. When the water evaporates, lower the heat.

6. **To make the dosais :** Pour a ladleful of batter over the tawa and spread quickly using a continous spiral motion, spreading it outwards till the dosai measures about 6 inches.

7. Increase the heat and cook for a couple of minutes till golden brown in colour.

8. Turn the dosai, carefully lifting the edges. Roast the potato masal and put in the center of the dosai and roast again for another couple of minutes till done.

9. Serve hot.

128

Milk Payasam
(Paal Payasam)

Ingredients
- 3 litres milk (skimmed milk)
- ¼ cup long-grained rice
- ½ cup sugar
- 6-8 cardamoms, crushed
- 1 teaspoon saffron

METHOD
1. Boil the milk with the rice in a heavy bottomed vessel.
2. Keep stirring till the milk reduces to half the quantity.
3. Add the sugar and crushed cardamoms.
4. Dissolve the saffron in half-cup warm milk and add the payasam
   Serve hot or chilled.

Ghia Dosa

Ingredients

- 1 cup rice soaked and then ground
- ¼ cup semolina.
- 1 ½ cups finely grated steamed marrow.
- 2 cups grated jaggery.
- A pinch a salt.

METHOD

1. Put little hot water into the jaggery and set aside till it dissolves.
2. Mix together all the above ingredients with enough milk to form a thick batter.
3. Now prepare the dosa.

130   Creamy Milk Pudding
(Basundi)

Ingredients

- 3 litres milk(skim milk)
- ½ cup sugar
- 1 teaspoon saffron
- 25gms raisins

METHOD

1. Bring the milk to the boil in a heavy bottomed vessel. Simmer till it thickens and gets reduced to one third the quantity.

2. Add the sugar and simmer for five more minutes.

3. Add the saffron.

   Serve chilled.

(Famous in all South India)

Semolina Laddu
(Rava Laddu)

131

Ingredients
- 1 ½ cups semolina, roasted
- 1 ½ cups sugar
- 2 tablespoons raisins

METHOD

1. Roast the semolina till light golden in colour.

2. Mix the sugar, roasted semolina powder fine in a dry grinder.

3. Shape into tight laddus.

4. The laddus can be stored in an airtight container for a few days.

132

Mango Halwa

Ingredients
- 4 ripe mangoes
- 4 cups skim milk
- 6 tblsps cardamom
- Silver warq

METHOD

1. Dissolve sugar in milk

2. Squeeze out the pulp of mangoes and put in a pan along with milk and caramoms and keep on stirring till the mixture turns thick and leaves the sides of the pan.

3. Put in thali, level the surface and cover with warq.

4. Set aside to turn cold and then cut into pieces.

5. Store in an airtight tin.

133

Sweet Idli

Ingredients

- ½ cup urad dhal.
- ¾ cup semolina
- 5 tblsps. finely grated jaggery,
- a big pinch soda bicarbonate
- pinch of salt.
- 25 gms of raisins
- 1 cup skim milk

METHOD

1. Soak dhal in water for a few hours.
2. Drain, grind to a paste and set aside for 4 hours.
3. Roast semolina on a dry gridle till it starts changing colour.
4. Then mix with dhal along with salt and soda.
5. Add enough milk to form a thick batter.
6. Mix in the rest of the above ingredients.
7. Steam idli katories nicely and fill half full with batter and steam till firm.
8. Serve hot.

134   Carrot Payasam

Ingredients

- 2 cups skim milk
- ½ cup each of grated carrots and sugar.
- ½ tsp cardamom powder
- 1 tblsp raisins.
- A few drops essence of rose
- Silver warq

METHOD

1. Dissolve sugar in milk
2. Cook the carrots in milk till the mixture turns thick.
3. Add raisins and rose essence.
4. Decorate with pieces of warq and serve hot.

135

Rice Payasam

Ingredients
- 1 cup broken rice.
- ¾ cup grated jaggery
- 1 cup skim milk
- 1 tsp cardamom powder

METHOD

1. Put 2 cups water in jaggery and prepare a syrup.
2. Peel and slice the mangoes, cook the mangoes in little water till soft, add syrup and cook till thick.
3. Heat to simmering, sprinkle cardmoms on top and serve hot.

136 Vermicelli Payasam
(Semiya Payasam)

Ingredients
- 2 litres milk (skim milk)
- ½ cup sugar
- 1 cup vermicelli
- 4 cardamoms, crushed
- ½ teaspoon saffron
- 25 gms raisins

METHOD

1. Boil the milk in a heavy bottomed vessel till it is reduced to ¾ the quantity.
2. Heat the karahi and roast the vermicelli till it turns reddish. Add to the milk which is being boiled.
3. Cook till the vermicelli is well done.
4. Add the sugar, crushed cardamoms and saffron.
5. Garnish with the raisins.
6. Serve hot or chilled.

Vermicelli Payasam

Sago Halwa

137   Sago Halwa

Ingredients

- 1 Cup Sago
- 2 Cup sugar
- a few drops orange red food coloring
- ½ tsp cardamom power.

METHOD

1 Soak sago in water for 1 hour.

2 Drain and add 1 ½ cups water and cook till it turns thick and leaves the sides of the pan.

3 Remove from fire and grind to a paste.

4. Put ½ cup water in sugar and prepare a thick syrup add the paste, colouring, cardamoms and cook till the mixture turns the thick.

5 Remove from fire and serve hot.

138

Stuffed Sweet Idli

Ingredients

- 1 cup each of urad dhal and rice
- a pinch each of soda bicarbonate and salt.

For stuffing

- 1 cup sugar
- 25 gms raisins, anjeer, khajur.
- 1 tsp cardamom powder

METHOD

1. Soak the rice and dhal for a few hours.
2. Drain and grind to a paste.
3. Mix in soda and salt and set aside for 3 hours.
4. Melt the sugar on a slow fire and mix in the filling ingredients.
5. Steam idli katories and half fill with cover with little more batter. Steam till set.

139 | Mango Kheer

Ingredients

- 4 ripe and sweet mangoes.
- 1 litre skim milk.
- ½ tsp saffron strands or its essence.
- 1 cup sugar
- 1 tsp cardamom powder

METHOD

1. Peel and extract juice from mangoes and beat till smooth.
2. Mix together milk and cardamoms and cook over a slow fire till the mixture thickens a little.
3. Add sugar and keep on stirring till it dissolves.
4. Mix in the essence of saffron or saffron after grinding them to a paste.

   Remove from fire, cool and mix in the fruit juice.

140 Khichdi

Ingredients

- 1 cup each of suji and bengal gram dhal
- 2 cups sugar
- 1 firm ripe banana, peeled and cut into thin rounds.
- 1 tsp cardamom powder
- 25 gms of raisins
- a little orange or pineapple juice.
- Silver foil.

METHOD

1. Sprinkle the cut banana pieces with orange or pineapple juices and set aside

2. Roast the dhal till light golden coloured.

3. Roast the rava to a pale brown colour.

4. Boil 4 cups of water and put in the dhal.

5. When it is half cooked, add the rava slowly and keep on stirring till the dhal is soft and mixture turns the thick.

6. Mix in the raisins and cardamom powder and remove from fire.

7. Put in steamed thali, level the surface and stick banana slices on it.

8. Cover with foil, cook and cut into small pieces

141 Mandagabe

Ingredients
- ½ cup each of rice flour and chana dhal
- 100 gms raisins
- 1 cup grated jaggery
- 1 tsp cardamom powder
- 1 cup skim milk

METHOD

1. Put in 1 ½ cups into the rice flour and mix well
2. In 3 cups water put dhal.
3. When dhal is cooked, add jaggery and 1 glass of water.
4. Mix well and cook till thick, put in the rice flour and keep on stirring till the mixture turns thick once again.
5. Put in the skim milk.
6. Sprinkle cardamom powder on top and serve at once.

142 Mint Chutney
(Pudina Thuvaiyal)

Ingredients

- 1 big bunch mint leaves
- 2 teaspoons mustard seeds
- 2 green chillies
- 2 red chillies
- ½ teaspoon asafoetida powder
- 3 teaspoons black gram dhal
- Marble-sized tamarind
- Salt to taste

METHOD

1. Stem the mint leaves and roast dry.

2. Roast the green chillies, red chillies, asafoetida powder, black gram dhal and mustard seeds till the black gram dhal turns golden.

3. Grind to a fine paste adding the roasted mint leaves, tamarind, salt and sufficient water.

4. Serve with hot rice, dosais and vadais.

143 Ridge Gourd Peel Chutney
(Peerkangai Tholi Thuvaiyal)

Ingredients
- ¼ kg ridge gourd
- 1 ½ tablespoons black gram dhal
- 1 tablespoon bengal gram dhal
- 2 teaspoons mustard seeds
- 1 ½ teaspoon asafoetida powder
- 3 green chillies
- 2 red chillies
- Marble-sized tamarind
- A small bunch coriander leaves
- Salt to taste

METHOD

1. Peel the ridge gourd. Chop the peel fine. Set aside.
2. Roast the black gram dhal, bengal gram dhal, mustard seeds, asafoetida powder, red chillies and green chillies. Set aside.
3. Roast the chopped ridge gourd peel for three to four minutes.
4. Blend everything to a paste in a liquidizer (mixie), adding the coriander leaves, tamarind, salt and a little water.
5. Serve with hot rice.

144 | Onion Chutney
(Vengaya Thuvaiyal)

Ingredients
- 3 onions, chopped fine
- 2 red chillies
- 3 green chillies
- 2 teaspoons mustard seeds
- 4 teaspoons black gram dhal
- ½ teaspoon asafoetida powder
- 1 small bunch coriander leaves
- Marble-sized tamarind
- Salt to taste

METHOD

1. Roast the red chillies, green chillies, mustard seeds, black gram dhal and asafoetida powder. Set aside.

2. Roast the chopped onions evenly till light golden in colour.

3. Grind everything to a fine paste in a liquidizer, adding coriander leaves, tamarind and salt.

4. Serve with hot rice.

145

Brinjal Chutney
(Kathirikkai Thuvaiyal)

Ingredients

- 1 big, round, purple brinjal
- 2 teaspoons mustard seeds
- 1 teaspoon asafoetida powder
- 2 tablespoons black gram dhal
- 6-7 green chillies
- 1 small lemon-sized tamarind
- 1 bunch coriander leaves
- Salt to taste

METHOD

1. Roast the brinjal on a naked flame till the skin is completely charred and the vegetable is soft. Skin mash well and set aside.

2. Roast the mustard seeds and asafetida powder.

3. Roast the black gram dhal separately and set aside.

4. Grind in a liquidizer the salt, tamarind, gree chillies, mustard seeds, asafoetida and coriander leaves. Add the mashed brinjal and blend for a minute or two.

5. Add the roasted black gram dhal and grind for a minute.
   Serve with rice.

Instant Mango Pickle
(Uppu Pisiri Mangai)

146

Ingredients
- 1 raw mango
- 2 teaspoons chilli powder
- ½ teaspoon turmeric powder
- 1 teaspoon asafoetida powder
- Salt to taste

For Tempering
- 2 teaspoons mustard seeds

METHOD

1. Peel and chop the mango to ½ inch pieces.
2. Mix the mango, salt, chilli powder, turmeric powder and asafoetida powder.
3. Roast the mustard seeds. When they splutter, add to the mango. Mix well.
4. Serve with rice and curd.

147 Grated Mango Pickle
(Mangai Thokku)

Ingredients

- 4 green mangoes (large variety)
- ¾ cup salt
- ¼ cup chilli powder
- 1 teaspoon fenugreek seeds
- 1 teaspoon asafoetida powder
- 2 teaspoons mustard seeds
- ½ teaspoon turmeric powder

METHOD

1. Peel and grate the mango. Set aside.

2. Roast dry the fenugreek seeds and asafoetida powder. Powder fine and set aside.

3. Heat the pan, add the mustard seeds. When they splutter, add the chilli powder, turmeric powder and sauté for a minute.

4. Add the grated mango, salt and fenugreek asafoetida powder.

5. Cool completely and store in a bottle.

Hot Lemon Pickle
(Elumichai Urugai)

148

Ingredients

- 6 lemons
- 8 tablespoons salt
- 4 teaspoons red chilli powder
- 6 green chillies, chopped to ½-inch size
- 1 ½ inch piece ginger, scraped and chopped fine
- 1 tablespoon fenugreek seeds
- ½ teaspoon asafoetida powder
- ½ teaspoon turmeric powder
- 1 teaspoon mustard seeds

METHOD

1. Roast dry the fenugreek seeds and asafoetida powder. Powder fine and set aside.
2. Boil the lemons whole, adding sufficient water to cover them.
3. Cool the lemons, quarter and set aside. Set aside also the cooked water.
4. Heat the pan add the mustard seeds. When they splutter, add the chilli powder, green chillies, ginger and turmeric powder. Fry for a minute or two.
5. Add the quartered lemons and the cooked water.
6. Add the salt and the fenugreek-asafoetida powder. Cook for a few minutes till everything blends well.
7. Store in an airtight bottle and refrigerate.

149

Green Chilli Pickle
(Milagai Thokku)

Ingredients

- 3 cups green chillies
- Large lemon-sized tamarind
- 2 tablespoons jaggery, powdered
- 2 teaspoons mustard seeds
- 1 big bunch coriander leaves
- Salt to taste

METHOD

1. Roast the mustard seeds. When they splutter, add the green chilies. Roast well.

2. Add the tamarind, powdered jaggery, Coriander leaves, and salt.

3. Grind to a coarse paste in a liquidizer (mixie). Do not use water.

4. Store in an airtight container.

5. This pickle will keep well for a week in a refrigerator.

6. Serve with dosais and curd rice.

150   Dried Chilli
(Moru Milagai)

Ingredients

- 4 cups green chillies,
- Slit sideways without removing the stalk
- 6 cups curd (skimmed)
- 4 cups salt
- 2 tablespoons fenugreek seeds

METHOD

1. Soak the fenugreek seeds in ½ cup water and grind to a fine paste.

2. Mix the curd with the salt and the fenugreek paste.

3. Soak the slit green chillies in the curd mixture for 3-4 days.

4. Shake the vessel every day.

5. On the fourth day, remove the green chillies and dry in the sun for the whole day. In the evening, resoak the partly dried green chillies in the curd mixture.

6. The following day remove the chillies and dry in the sun once again. Resoak them in the evening. Continue this process every day till all the curd mixture is completely absorbed.

7. Dry the green chillies in the sun till they turn cream in colour.

8. Store in an airtight container and use when required.

9. Serve with curd rice.

151 Tomato Onion Chutney

Ingredients

- 100gms tomato
- 100gms onion
- 2 nos. green chillies
- 1 nos. red chillies
- 1 tb spoon blackgram dhal
- 1 tb spoon bengal gram dhal
- 1 pinch asofoetida
- 10 gms tamarind
- Salt to taste

METHOD

1. Roast asofoetida, black gram dhal and bengal gram dhal along with green chillies, red chillies and onion.

2. Add tomato and cook till soft.

3. Add tamarind and allow to simmer for few more minutes.

4. Add salt to taste and grind all the ingredients together.

Tamarind Juice
(Pulli Thannner)

Ingredients
- Lemon sized tamarind
- 1 cup warm water

METHOD

1. Soak the tamarind in warm water for about 10 minutes.

2. Squeeze and extract the maximum juice from the pulp. Keep adding water if necessary.

Sambar Powder
(Sambar Podi)

Ingredients

- 1 ¾ cups coriander seeds
- 2 cups red chillies
- ¼ cup cumin seeds
- 1 ½ tablespoon fenugreek seeds
- 1 ½ tablespoon peppercorns
- 1 ½ tablespoon mustard seeds
- 2 teaspoon turmeric powder
- 2 teaspoon bengal gram dhal
- 2 teaspoon red gram dhal
- 2 teaspoon poppy seeds
- 2 large sticks cinnamon
- a few curry leaves

METHOD

1. Roast dry all the ingredients separately, till they give off strong aroma.(Do not roast turmeric powder).

2. Finely, powder all the ingredients together.

3. Store in an airtight container and use when required.

Rasam Powder
(Rasam Podi)

Ingredients
- 2 ½ cups coriander seeds
- 1 ¼ cups red chillies
- ½ cup peppercorns
- ¾ cup red gram dhal
- ¼ cup bengal gram dhal
- ½ table cumin seeds
- 1 teaspoon turmeric powder
- 1 small bunch curry leaves

METHOD

1. Roast dry all the ingredients separately, except the turmeric powder.
2. Mix all the ingredients, powder fine in a liquidizer adding the turmeric powder.
3. Store in an airtight container and use when required.

Mysore Rasam Powder
(Mysore Rasam Podi)

Ingredients
- 2 cups coriander seeds
- ½ cup peppercorns
- ¼ cup cumin seeds
- 4 teaspoons fenugreek seeds
- 1 bunch curry leaves
- 2 cups red chillies
- 2 teaspoons turmeric powder

METHOD

1. Roast dry the coriander seeds, peppercorns, cumin seeds, fenugreek seeds and curry leaves till they give off a strong aroma. Set aside.

2. Roast the red chillies.

3. Powder fine the above ingredients together, adding the turmeric powder.

4. Store in an airtight container and use when required.

Curry Powder
(Cury Podi)

Ingredients

- 1 ¼ cups coriander seeds
- ¾ cup bengal gram dhal
- ½ up black gram dhal
- ¾ cup red chillies
- 2 teaspoons asafoetida powder
- Marble-sized tamarind
- Salt to taste

METHOD

1. Roast dry the coriander seeds, bengal gram dhal and black gram dhal.

2. Roast the red chillies.

3. Mix all the ingredients together and powder almost fine. This powder is used for poriyals like Colocasia Roast etc.

4. Store the powder in an airtight container and use when required.

Dosai Chilli Powder
(Dosai Milagai Podi)

Ingredients

- 1 ¼ cups red chillies
- ½ cup black gram dhal
- ½ cup bengal gram dhal
- ¼ cup sesame seeds
- 1 teaspoon asafoetida powder
- 2 tablespoons jaggery, powdered
- Marble-sized tamarind (optional)
- Salt to taste

METHOD

1. Roast the red chillies.
2. Roast dry the black gram dhal, bengal gram dhal, asafoetida powder and sesame seeds.
3. Mix all the ingredients and powder coarse. Add the salt. It makes an excellent accompaninent to dosais and idlis.

Glossary of
South Indian Recipes

- **Adai:** Rice, Blackgram dhal, Bengal gram dhal and Red gram dhal are roasted and ground to coarse paste along with salt, ginger, chillies and asoefotida. They are then made like pancakes and served hot.

- **Avail:** This is a mix of vegetables (Pumpkin, Drum sticks, Beans, Carrot, Unripe banana and Yam) which are garnished with green chillies and curd.

- **Bath:** Bath is rice based recipe which is seasoned with spices. There are various baths made of tomato, brinjal and lemon.

- **Chutney:** It is paste made up of different vegetables singly or along with a pulse/pulses or cereals. They are usually garnished with coriander leaves, curry leaves and pudina.

- **Dosai:** It is made up of any cereal and pulse (mainly rice and black gram dhal). First, a batter is made of the ingredients and it is spread over a Tava and cooked to make a pan cake. This is popularly called a Dosa.

- **Elumichampazha** — Lemon

- **Idli:** This is made of a cereal and pulse combination. A batter is prepared and is steam cooked which is then served with chutney or sambar.

- **Inji** — Ginger

- **Kosumbari:** This is a kind of dhal and lentil salad where the dhals are soaked overnight and are garnished with coriander and green chillies.

- **Kootu:** One or two kinds of vegetables are boiled and are garnished.

- **Kuzhambu:** This preparation is similar to sambar but is made without any vegetables.

- **Mangai**   — Mango
- **Moru**   — Buttermilk
- **Ogaray:** Ogaray is rice based recipe which is garnished with either mango or black gram or mustard.

- **Payasam:** Payasam is a sweet dish which is very similar to sweet pongal but has a liquid consistency as compared to sweet pongal.

- **Podi:** Podi is a combination of lentils and spices which are roasted and ground together into a fine powder. This can be used as a ready to eat accompanying dish with idli or dosa.

- **Pongal:** Pongal is a combination of rice and green gram dhal (Moong) seasoned with pepper and zeera (hot Pongal). Rice and green gram cooked and seasoned with jaggery and cardamom is known as sweet pongal.

- **Pappu**   — Dhal
- **Poriyal:** Poriyal means vegetables which are roasted.

- **Rasam:** Rasam is a dish made with tamarind water or tomato water which are seasoned with pepper, curry leaves, garlic, asoefitida.

- **Sambar:** Sambar is a blend of dhal with tamarind juice and vegetables along with special masala comprising of dhaniya, Bengal gram, asafetida, red chillies, curry leaves and zeera.

- **Thuvaiyal:** This is a kind of chutney which can be made with pudina or ridge gourd or onion or brinjal but the consistency of the chutney is very thick.

- **Vengaya**   — Small onion

Glossary of food items in different languages

ENGLISH	HINDI	TAMIL	KANNADA	MALAYALAM	TELUGU
Amaranath Leaves	Chholai–ka–Saag	Mulai Keerai	Mulla Dantu	Mullan Cheru- Cheera	Mulla – Thotakoora
Aniseed	Saunf	Sombu			
Asafoeteda	Hing	Perungayam	Hingu	Yangu	Ingua
Ashgourd	Petha	Poosanikai	Budagumbala. mashaalyal	Kumbalanga	Boodida gummadi
Banana (Raw)	Kela	Vazhaikkai	Bale. Hannu	Vazhapazham	Arati Pandu
Bay Leaves	Tej Patta	Brinji ilai			
Beans, Cluster	Gwar Ki Palli	Kotha Varangai	Gori koyi	Kotha vara	Goruchikkudu
Beaten Rice	Chiwada	Aval			
Beet root	Chukandar	Beet root			Beet
Bengal gram flour	Besan	Kadalaiparupu			
Bitter gourd	Karela	Pagarkai pabakkai	Hagal	Kaippakka	Kakarakayi
Black gram Dhal	Urad Dhal	Ulutham Parupu	Uddina Bele	Uzhunnu parippu	Minapapappu
Brinjal/ Aubergine	Baingan	Kathrikkai	Badane	Bazhuthininga	Vankaya
Butter milk	Lassi/ Mattha	Moru	Majjige	Chuakuduad	Majjiga
Cabbage	Band Gobhi	Muttaikos	Kosu	Muttagose	Goskoora

ENGLISH	HINDI	TAMIL	KANNADA	MALAYALAM	TELUGU
Capsicum	Simla Mirch	Kudamilagi	Menasinakaya	Mulaku	Mirapakayai
Carrot	Gajar	Carrot	Gajjare		Gajjara
Cauliflower	Fool gobhi	Kovippu, Cauli flower	Hukosu		
Chick peas	Kabuli Channa	Kothu Kadalai			
Green Chilly	Hari Mirch	Pachaimilagai			
Red Chilly	Lal Mirch	Vattral Millagai			
Chow Chow	Chow Chow	Seemai Kathirikkai, chow chow	Seeme badane		Seemavankaya
Cinnamon	Dal chini	Rawanga pattai			Chamadumpa
Cloves	Lawang	Krambu			Kothimiri
Colocasia	Arbi	Chepangkizhahngu	Samagadde	Chembu	Dhni yalu
Coriander Leaves	Hara Dhania	Kotha Mallai	Kothambari sappu	Kothamalli	Dosakayi
Coriander seeds	Dhania	Kothamalliverai	Kothambari	Kothambalari	Jeelakorra
Cucumber	Kheera	Vellarikkai	Southekayi	Vellarikka	Perugu
Cumin seeds	Jeera	Jeeragam	Jeerage	Kothamvalari	Karivepaku
Curd	Dahi	Thayir	Mosaru	Thayir	
Curry Leaves	Curry patta	Karivepilai	Karibevu	Karivepilai	
Dry ginger	Saunth	Chukku			
Drum sticks	Sahjan	Murungakkai	Nuggeyele	Muringaela	Mulagaakulu
Fenugreek seeds	Methi	Vendayam	Menthya	Uluva	Menthikoora
Garlic	Lassun	Poondu	Belluli	Vellulli	Vellulli
Gherkaisn	Kundru	Kovakkai			
Ginger	Adrakh	Inji			

Zero Oil South Indian Cook Book ——————————————— |209|

ENGLISH	HINDI	TAMIL	KANNADA	MALAYALAM	TELUGU
Green gram Dhal	Moong Dhal	Payapham parupu	Hesarabele	Cheru payar parippu	Pesara pappu
Jaggery	Gur	Vellam			
Kohlradi	Knol khol	Knol khol			
Ladies figers/okra	Bhindi	Vendaikkai	Vende	Vandakkai	Vandakayi
Lime/lemon	Nimbu	Elumichampazham	Nimbe	Cherunaranga	Nimmapandu
Mango (green)	Aam	Manga	Mavinakayi	Manga	Mamidikayi
Mango (ripe)	aam	Mampazham	Mabinahannu	Mampazham	Mamidipandu
Milk	Doodh	Paal			
Mint	pudhina	Pudhina	Pudhina	Pudhina	Pudhina
Mustard seeds	Rai	Kadugu	Agasi	Cheruchana	Avise ginzalu
Nutmeg	Jaiphal	Jhadhikkai	Jajikiyi	Jathikkai	Jajikayi
Onion	Pyaz	Vengayam	Eerulli	Ulli	Neerulli
Onion, small (shallot)	Pyaz	China vengayam sambhar			
Omum	Ajwayain	Omum	Uma	Ayamothakm	Bamu
Parvoiled Rice	Usna chaval	Puzhungal arisi	Kusuvalakki	Puzhungal ari	Uppudu Biyyam
Peas	Mutter	Pattani	Batani	Pattani	Batani
Pepper Black	Kali Mirch	Milagu	-	-	-
Poppy Seeds	Khas-Khas	Khasa-Khasa	Afim	Afiam	Gasagusalu
	Posta				
Potato	Alu	Urulaikizhangu	Alugadda	Urula Kizhangu	Alu gaddalu
Radish	Mooli	Mullangi	Mullangi	Mullangi	Mullangi
Ragi	Madua	Kezhvaragu	Ragi	Moothari	Ragulu
Raisins	Kishmish	Dhratchai	Drakshi	Mundiringa	Kishmish
Red gram dal	Arhar dhal	Tuvaram parupu	Thugare bele	Tuvara parippu	Kandi Pappu

ENGLISH	HINDI	TAMIL	KANNADA	MALAYALAM	TELUGU
Refined flour	Maida	Maida			
Rice	Chaval	Arisi	Akki	Ari	Biyyam
Ridge Gourd	Torai	Peerkangai	Heeraikhi	Peechinga	Beerakayi
Saffron	Kessar	Kungumappu			
Sago	Sabudana	Javvarisi	Sabbakki	Sago	Saggu
Salt	Namak	Uppu			
Semolina	Rava / sŏoji	Ravai	Rava	Rava	Rava
Snake Gourd	Chachinda	Pudalangi	Padavala	Pavavalanga	Potlakayi
Sugar	Cheeni	Chakkarai	Sakkare	Panchasara	Pancha dara
Sugar Syrup	Sheera	Chakkarai Pagu			
Tamorind	Imli	Puli	Hunise	Puli	Chiutha pandu
Tapioca	Simla Alu	Mera valli kizhangu			
Tomato	Tamatar	Thakkali		Takkali	Takkali
Turmeric	Haldi	Manjal	Anashina	Manjal	Pasupu
Vermicelli	Sewian	Semiya	Shevize	Somiya	Somiya
Wheat	Gehum	Godumai	Godhi	Gendum	Godhumalu
Whole Wheat Flour	Atta	Godumai Mavu	Godhi Hittu	Gothambu	Godhuma
Yam	Jimikand / Sooram	Chenai Kizhangu	Suvarna gadde	Chna	Kanda dumpa